THE MILITARY AUSTIN TEN

ARJAN VAN DER HOEK

AMBERLEY

First published 2025

Amberley Publishing
The Hill, Stroud,
Gloucestershire, GL5 4EP

www.amberley-books.com

ISBN: 978 1 3981 2467 7 (print)
ISBN: 978 1 3981 2468 4 (ebook)

British Library Cataloguing in Publication Data.
A catalogue record for this book is available from the British Library.

Typeset in 10pt on 13pt Celeste.
Origination by Amberley Publishing.
Printed in the UK.

Contents

Acknowledgements

Following the purchase of my Austin Tilly and saloon in 2004 and 2005, a journey began during which I had the pleasure of meeting several new people. Fortunately, this has become easier thanks to the digital world we live in, but a face-to-face meeting is always different. Without these 'first contacts' with Michael Shackleton and John Simpson of The Tilly Register, I probably would not have been able to put this book together. When I first joined the Register, they enabled me to learn more about the Tillys, collect information, and continue to expand my knowledge. Michael gave his support and edited the first draft.

In previous years, another Dutchman led the way in the world of military vehicle publishing. He had a soft spot for Tillys, just like me. The late Bart Vanderveen had already researched and described the four Tillys in *Wheels & Tracks* magazine, particularly the Austin which was featured in issue 63.

I would like to thank Jan Bonthond. Without his efforts as a car restorer, my Austins would have looked very different, or perhaps would not even be in my possession anymore.

One of my personal goals has always been to share information as much as possible. This has been done by digitising the various manuals I own, and also by writing articles. I was therefore very pleased when The Tilly Register was approached by Amberley Publishing to ask if anyone would be interested in writing a book about Tillys. After restoring my Austins, I had already considered this idea. I would like to thank Amberley Publishing for giving me the opportunity to write this book about the military Austin 10 during the Second World War.

Finally, I must thank my family for listening to me talk about the Austins over all these years. My dad supported me when I bought the Austin Tilly. My lovely wife, Corrie, without whom I would probably not have bought the Austin saloon. Although initially intended as a donor car, it eventually became the next restoration project.

Introduction

The Austin 10 Model 1939 Saloon and the Austin 10 Light Utility Truck (affectionately known as the 'Tilly') both stand as iconic symbols of British automotive ingenuity during the tumultuous years of the Second World War and beyond. This book describes the origins of these vehicles, exploring their design, development, and deployment during wartime. Furthermore, it highlights their roles in various military operations, as well as their enduring legacy in the post-war era, showcasing their contributions to civilian life and industry.

The Austin Tilly is the best-known example of the various makes of light utility trucks. Hillman, Morris and Standard also produced these small trucks, but Austin manufactured them in greater numbers. Of this make, surviving vehicles are regarded as the 'Tilly' by the general public. It was used by the British armed forces from 1940 until the mid-1950s. During its service, the Austin was deployed to many, but not all, divisions of the military. After its use in the military, many Tillys found their way into civilian life, where they were used until the end of their lifespan. While some were stored or left abandoned, many ended up in local scrapyards.

As popular interest in military vehicles increased during the 1970s, attention was initially focused on the Jeep and other American vehicles. However, since the beginning of this century, the Austin Tilly has been rediscovered as the precious vehicle it truly is. Thanks to The Tilly Register, there is now a dedicated information point for enthusiasts. Every year, the number of surviving Austin Tillys has grown as more have come to light. The demand for military vehicles, other than the well-known Jeep, led to the rediscovery of both the Tilly and the saloon. The Austin is the most produced and therefore most common, and very popular as an alternative to the Jeep. In some ways, this is a form of revenge, as the American Jeep was the vehicle that replaced many Tillys during the war.

1

Austins for the British Armed Forces

Before we focus on the small Austin military vehicles, this book begins with a chapter about the Austin Motor Company. The Austin Motor Company had a long history of delivering several vehicles to the British armed forces. During the First World War, Austin produced armoured cars. Demand for cars declined during the war, so the Austin Motor Company also produced shells, aeroplanes, and ambulances. After the war, the Austin Seven two-seater Light Car was produced from 1922. A special War Department type of the Austin Seven was used by the British Army. Other Austins in service were the Austin 10 and 12 HP, 16 HP, and 20 HP saloon cars. These last vehicles were used as staff cars. The Austin 10, as an open tourer, was also used as a Wireless Car for communications for the army.

Second World War Effort

At the time of the outbreak of the Second World War on 3 September 1939, the British motor industry was already involved in the production of equipment and vehicles for the army. In 1939, plans were made for the British Expeditionary Force (BEF) to go to France, initially sending some 25,000 vehicles across the Channel. From the ports of Nantes, Brest, and Saint-Nazaire, British troops were concentrated in the area between Arras and Amiens. Slowly, the number of vehicles built up to around 85,000. The 1939–40 BEF campaign is well documented, including the withdrawal from Dunkirk and other ports. Eventually, 5,000 vehicles were evacuated. The remainder had to be left behind, including at least a number of Austin 10s, including saloons and, most likely, the first model of the Austin Tilly.

1940 was the first full year of the war and production of civilian cars decreased to just under 2,000 units. The total number of cars on British roads was 1,348,817, almost 280,000 lower than in 1939. The number of hackney carriages in use, however, had increased by over 14,000 to 81,484. Many cars were commandeered by the armed forces, and others were converted into ambulances, canteen vans, and the like. Some manufacturers supplied military versions of their civilian cars directly to the War Office, the Admiralty, and other government authorities.

In 1939, fewer than half a million people were employed by the motor industry, building and repairing motor vehicles in the United Kingdom. The peak of employment was in 1943, when the number had risen to over 1.1 million. Half of these were part-time female workers. Many garages around the country were also involved in the maintenance and overhaul of military vehicles. They were also involved in the assembly of Lend-Lease vehicles, which arrived in kit form from North America.

With the exception of the last six months of 1945, 1941–45 was a period of almost entirely wartime production for car makers. Most vehicles were military trucks of various types. Many of the manufacturers were engaged in a wide variety of equipment. In May 1945, the war ended and production for the armed services was soon scaled down as the motor industry gradually began to produce civilian models once again. To ease production, many of the 1939/40 models were reintroduced, but often with minor changes to the details.

Longbridge War Years, 1939–45

It is commonly believed that, during the war, car manufacturers simply continued producing cars, supplying them exclusively to the government for military purposes. This, however, is far from the truth. Motor vehicles were still being produced during the war.

End of the assembly line at the Austin factory at Longbridge. Saloons and ambulances stand side by side. (Author's collection)

In a typical peacetime year, Longbridge would manufacture nearly 100,000 vehicles, including cars ranging from 8 hp to 28 hp and commercial vehicles such as small vans and 3-ton trucks, as well as industrial and marine engines.

It is not surprising, then, that Austin vehicles played a significant role in meeting the transportation needs of the British Army during the war. Every week, up to 500 military and other vehicles were produced, including four-wheel-drive and six-wheel-drive vehicles, army breakdown trucks, fire-fighting vehicles, ambulances, RAF tenders, troop carriers, and signal and workshop units. By the end of the war, more than 120,000 of these vehicles had been produced. The Civil and National Fire Services were equipped with more than 5,000 Austin 2-ton lorries in various configurations. Longbridge also produced around 20,000 industrial engines, nearly half of which were paired with fire pumps.

In the months leading up to the declaration of war, production at Longbridge gradually shifted to meet the needs of the armed forces. This shift had to be carefully balanced with the continued demand for civilian goods. By September 1939, the factory's infrastructure was ready. One of the first tasks was to camouflage the factory and, although this had been planned in advance, the entire operation was completed in just three days. From the air, the factory's 120-acre roof blended seamlessly into the surrounding countryside. The Lickey Hills, near the factory, provided a panoramic view, and observers were amazed at how the factory seemed to disappear into the landscape, even with a road running across the site.

Austin saloon on the production line where the body is mounted on the chassis at the Austin factory. (Author's collection)

The wartime environment was challenging, as civilian production needed to continue alongside preparations for war. At Longbridge, a flight shed was constructed in 1937, marking the beginning of non-vehicle production, including aircraft. The first aircraft built there was the Fairey Battle and, in September 1938, it became the first plane to take off from the site.

The range of products and components manufactured at Longbridge was staggering. The site produced everything from simple machined shafts to complete Lancaster bombers. Some wartime products were large, while others were small, but all were essential to the war effort. In addition to land vehicles, Longbridge contributed to the war in the air with a remarkable array of aircraft products. As well as Lancasters, these included balloon cable cutters, Beaufighter aircraft and Miles Master wing and centre sections, and Horsa glider fuselages, totalling 5,000 aircraft. Austin also produced 15,000 oil and fuel tanks for four-engine bombers, utilising 2.5 million square feet of light alloy. The site manufactured numerous other components, such as landing gear parts and components for Rolls-Royce engines and Rotol propellers.

Among other necessities produced during the war were service helmets made by the Austin presses, totalling 500,000 units. The jerrican, which facilitated the safe storage and easy pouring of fuel, was another notable design that should have won an award. Over 110,000 bogey suspension units and a large number of Churchill tank driving gear were also produced. While most of Longbridge's production focused on the army and air force, parts were also made for the Royal and Merchant navies. This included 440,000 mine mechanism plates and depth-charge pistols, as well as over 110,000 magazines for the naval Oerlikon gun.

Although many of the items produced were large, there were also small but vital items, such as tail fins for 250-lb, 1,000-lb, and 4,000-lb bombs. In addition, approximately 300,000 Vickers and Hispano machine-gun magazines were manufactured for aircraft armament. One of the smaller items produced was the bilge pump, which was included with every airborne lifeboat on a bomber.

For the land war, in addition to vehicle production, Longbridge produced 1.35 million rounds of armour-piercing ammunition in 2-pounder, 6-pounder, and 10-pounder sizes, along with 3.35 million ammunition boxes. Magazines for machine guns, including those for the Bren, Sten, and other models, totalled over 4 million units.

2

Origins of the Austin 10

The Austin 10 represented a significant advancement in automotive design, incorporating features such as a robust chassis and mechanical brakes. Its compact size, coupled with a relatively spacious interior, made it popular among families and businesses alike. As tensions rose in Europe during the late 1930s, almost all car manufacturers produced a car in the '10' format. It was a very popular type. The Austin 10, or 10/4, was introduced as an entirely new model in April 1932, and it quickly replaced the Seven as the best-selling Austin. The Austin 10 Saloon was, in fact, a small 'large' four-door car, which could comfortably accommodate four passengers. The Austin 10, also known as the 10 HP, was introduced as the Model GC Saloon. It was a closed car with four doors and a 1,125-cc side-valve engine with only 10 horsepower.

The 10 was a typical Austin: rugged, reliable, and cheap to run, elegant but not flashy. The range was expanded with a two-seater Tourer with a rear dickey seat, and a four-door open tourer, a convertible, and a van. Special bodies were also built for the Austin 10 by the Flewitt, Gordon and Patrick company. Major improvements were regularly made throughout the 10's career. With the arrival of the Cambridge in 1936, the Austin 10 became even more spacious, and also somewhat heavier.

A pre-war Austin 10 model from 1938. (Kuine's Military Photography)

Introducing the New Austin 10

New Austin designs were introduced in 1939. The Austin 8 came first in February 1939. It was announced by Lord Austin that the new car marked the second stage of the Austin Prosperity Programme for 1939. A range of commercial vehicles was the first stage. In his speech, Lord Austin mentioned the continued talk of possibilities of war in an article in the *Motor* magazine of 28 February 1939.

Regarding the new car, Austin aimed at a very big production schedule per week, in addition to a large output of higher-powered models. They estimated that during the next six months, their purchases of materials and plant alone would amount to at least £4,000,000. In the six months previously, no less than £3,000,000 was spent on materials and plant.

The Austin 10 GRQ was a product of British automotive ingenuity. It was based on the popular Austin 10 series, which had been in production since the mid-1930s. It was built on a sturdy chassis with a four-cylinder engine. GRQ stood for reliability and versatility. The newly developed Austins had a semi-self-carrying body in several models: the Saloon (sedan), Tourer (open top), and Van (delivery). The body was bolted to the floor, so the body shell was structurally integrated with the floor. This gave the car a semi-unitary (or monocoque) structure. If the body had been welded to the floor, it would have been a unitary (one-piece) structure.

Cover of *The Light Car* magazine, June 1939. (Author's collection)

Shortly after the introduction, the Second World War began in May 1939. This caused large changes throughout the automotive industry. All car manufacturers, Austin Motor Company included, would produce cars, trucks, and more in the next five years for the war effort. A large quantity of different models was produced in those years. Production of the Austin truck models exceeded 90,000 trucks. These trucks varied from ambulances, 4x4 and 6x6 models. Also, the smaller Austin 8 was made for the War Department in the Saloon and Tourer (AP) models. Austin produced approximately 50,000 cars in the models 8, 10, 12, and 16.

A New Designer

The personal car line of the Austin Motor Company was completely redesigned by Argentinian-born Ricardo 'Dick' Burzi, who joined Austin from Lancia. Ricardo Burzi was a car designer. His best-known work was for Austin Motor Company in Birmingham. Burzi was born in Buenos Aires, Argentina, and in 1929 he worked for Lancia in Italy. He was forced to leave because he drew a cartoon about Benito Mussolini – his cartoons were published in some newspapers. Initially, Lancia moved him to their body builder in Paris. Here, he was discovered by Lord Austin, who recruited him to work at Longbridge. Lord Austin had received a recommendation from Vincenzo Lancia during a boat trip to the United States on the *Queen Mary*.

On his arrival at Longbridge, Burzi spoke no English, but was soon known as 'Dick'. His first designs for the Austin 16 were too progressive for the conservative British. In 1938, Burzi was appointed Head of Styling by Leonard Lord. Due to Burzi's Italian background, he was interned on the Isle of Man when Italy entered the Second World War. He was released in 1943 and began designing the Austin A40.

Ricardo 'Dick' Burzi.

Advert for the new Austin 10. (Author's collection)

3

The Austin 10 Saloon (GRQ)

The new Austin 10 was advertised in the brochure as a car with a sparkling performance and a superb appearance:

> Motoring finds its newest thrill in a masterpiece amongst light cars. Easy to look at and even easier to ride in, this new 10 provides the roomiest accommodation for four persons and affords wide-angle vision. For economy and dependability, it is every inch an Austin – for all-round satisfaction it stands alone.

The 'new' Austin 10 started in May 1939 with chassis number 177363.

The Austin 10 GRQ featured a robust construction designed to withstand the rigours of off-road travel. Its adaptation for military operations in diverse terrains would become the Austin 10 Light Utility Truck. This latter vehicle was designated as the Austin 10 GYG, but would be commonly known as one of the four makes of Tilly.

The middle pages of the brochure for the Austin 10 Saloon 1939. You can see that the number plate holder is under the rear bumper. (Author's collection)

The new Austin 10 Saloon, as announced, was produced in just four colours: black with brown upholstery, maroon with maroon upholstery, Bluebird blue with Bluebird blue upholstery, and royal blue with blue upholstery. However, the Austin 10 Tourer was only delivered in three colours (not in royal blue).

The new Austins featured a novel 'alligator' bonnet, a horizontal grille, and a one-piece bonnet. They had rapid acceleration, positive steering, and powerful braking. This car was ready for modern traffic conditions, and cost just £175 for a saloon with a fixed head, and £185 for a sliding-head saloon (with sunroof).

According to the brochure, there were no two-tone versions. These two-tone painted Austins probably appeared post-war. The mudguards, bonnet and roof are then painted in another colour in contrast to the body. After the war, the Austin 10 was built until 1947 until it was replaced by the Austin A40 Devon.

Cover of the brochure for the Austin 10 Saloon 1939. (Author's collection)

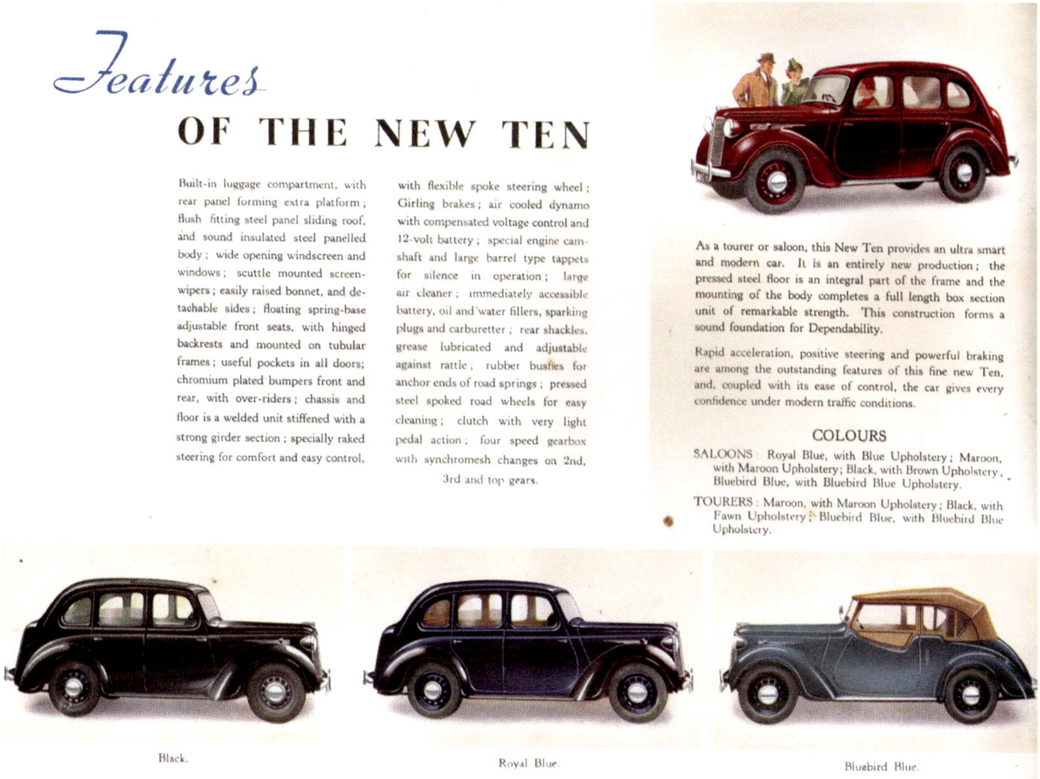
Features OF THE NEW TEN

Built-in luggage compartment, with rear panel forming extra platform; flush fitting steel panel sliding roof, and sound insulated steel panelled body; wide opening windscreen and windows; scuttle mounted screen-wipers; easily raised bonnet, and detachable sides; floating spring-base adjustable front seats, with hinged backrests and mounted on tubular frames; useful pockets in all doors; chromium plated bumpers front and rear, with over-riders; chassis and floor is a welded unit stiffened with a strong girder section; specially raked steering for comfort and easy control, with flexible spoke steering wheel; Girling brakes; air cooled dynamo with compensated voltage control and 12-volt battery; special engine cam-shaft and large barrel type tappets for silence in operation; large air cleaner; immediately accessible battery, oil and water fillers, sparking plugs and carburetter; rear shackles, grease lubricated and adjustable against rattle; rubber bushes for anchor ends of road springs; pressed steel spoked road wheels for easy cleaning; clutch with very light pedal action; four speed gearbox with synchromesh changes on 2nd, 3rd and top gears.

As a tourer or saloon, this New Ten provides an ultra smart and modern car. It is an entirely new production; the pressed steel floor is an integral part of the frame and the mounting of the body completes a full length box section unit of remarkable strength. This construction forms a sound foundation for Dependability.

Rapid acceleration, positive steering and powerful braking are among the outstanding features of this fine new Ten, and, coupled with its ease of control, the car gives every confidence under modern traffic conditions.

COLOURS

SALOONS: Royal Blue, with Blue Upholstery; Maroon, with Maroon Upholstery; Black, with Brown Upholstery; Bluebird Blue, with Bluebird Blue Upholstery.

TOURERS: Maroon, with Maroon Upholstery; Black, with Fawn Upholstery; Bluebird Blue, with Bluebird Blue Upholstery.

Black. Royal Blue. Bluebird Blue.

Brochure showing the different types and colours of the Austin 10 Saloon 1939. (Author's collection)

Road Test

In the section entitled *Features and Specifications* (see image above) you can read how the Austin Car Company recommended the new Austin 10 in its own brochure. The magazine *The Light Car* of 22 September 1939 contained a more independent road test of the Austin. All publicity photos show the Austin 10 Saloon with licence plate FOC 511. The road test was made and assessed with this particular Austin.

The summary of the road test was:

> Ranked as one of the most popular family cars in the country, the Austin 10 was subject to considerable revision and improvements. Although the Austin remained basically conventional (for that time) in design, it incorporated a large number of updated features. It was modern, but not freakishly ultra-modern, and created the atmosphere in the Austin tradition of dependability and comfort.
>
> According to the road test, comfort was the keyword. The front seats are shaped to fit the human anatomy. Even for long-distance trips, they are comfortable. In the rear, the seats provide comfortable accommodation for two people.
>
> The controls on the dashboard are laid out with a view to the driver's convenience. The large speedo is on the right, and a dial combining ammeter, oil gauge and

The Light Car

Road Tests of 1940 Models

THE AUSTIN TEN

In Its Latest Form, It is a Car Which Appeals Particularly to the Family Man

IN BRIEF

THE AUSTIN MOTOR CO., LTD.

AUSTIN TEN ROAD TEST

Road test article, *The Light Car* magazine. (Author's collection)

petrol gauge is on the left of the steering column. [Nowadays some owners add a temperature gauge to the dashboard.]

The visibility in all directions is unusually good. There are three side windows on each side, two rear windows and a wide windscreen providing a clear view in all directions.

At the rear, the luggage accommodation is adequate. The door panels provide room for maps and gloves. Behind the rear squab, the wide shelf provides room for parcels and other similar objects. The rear luggage boot is large and the lid folds down to carry more luggage, if required. The spare wheel is carried in the same compartment, under a shelf.

Maintenance should give little trouble. The opened bonnet gives easy access to components such as battery, carburettor and radiator filler.

The final question was how the Austin 10 performed on the road. The brief answer was: 'In a very satisfactory fashion'.

During the test, the Austin achieved an impressive top speed of 63 mph and an acceleration of 25.2 secs over the standing quarter mile. One of the most engaging features is the flexibility in top gear. Main-road hills of appreciable gradient can be taken in top gear without any slacking of speed. At 50 mph it is definitely good.

The capacity of the engine to pull is steady at low speeds when steep gradients are tackled. It gave the promise that the car will deal even with a temporary overload, without giving cause to worry. Throughout its speed range, the engine is commendably quiet and, incidentally there is a pleasing absence of wind noise from the body. The gearbox was not so quiet on the indirect ratios, particularly second. Shifting gear deserved a praise. You had to be clumsy to miss a change between any of the three upper ratios, provided with synchromesh. The clutch is very light in operation.

The suspension is one of the best at the moment it was tested in 1939. For a car with a wheelbase of 7 ft 9½ inches, to travel so smoothly over the bad surfaces speaks well for the skill of the Austin engineers. There is a complete freedom from bounce at the back, which greatly adds to the comfort of passengers in the rear. The absence of roll gives the driver a feeling of confidence.

The orthodox suspension system with long, supple semi-elliptic springs all around, the double-acting, piston-type hydraulic shock-absorbers, are fitted at both front and rear. Those at the front are set transversely in order to act in some measure as anti-roll devices. This contributes to the good behaviour of the car in corners. The steering is fairly high geared, but light. A bare two turns of the steering wheel, moves the wheels from full lock to full lock, making manoeuvring in confined spaces easy and gives complete control at higher speeds.

The brakes, made by Girling, were praised for their smoothness of operation and power. The brake test was taken at 32 mph on a Ferodo-Tapley meter, resulting in a reading of 92 per cent. The car would probably have come to a full stop in a straight line without a hand on the steering wheel if this was done on a road.

Features and Specifications

The complete features of the new Austin 10 were as follows: built-in luggage compartment with rear panel forming an extra platform; flush-fitting steel panel sliding roof and sound-insulated steel-panelled body; wide-opening windscreen and windows; scuttle-mounted windscreen wipers; easily raised bonnet with detachable sides; floating spring-base adjustable seats with hinged backrest, mounted on tubular frames; useful pockets in all doors; chromium bumpers front and rear with over-riders; chassis and floor is a bolted unit stiffened with a strong girder section; specially raked steering for comfort and easy control with flexible, spoked steering wheel; Girling brakes; air-cooled dynamo with compensated voltage control and 12-volt battery; special engine camshaft and large barrel-type tappets for silencer in operation; large air cleaner; immediately accessible battery, oil and water filters, sparking plugs, and carburettor; rear shackles, grease-lubricated and adjustable against rattle, rubber bushes for anchor ends of road springs; pressed-steel spoked road wheels for easy cleaning; clutch with very light pedal action; and four-speed gearbox with synchromesh changes on second, third, and top gears. The engine side valves are on the nearside, and the pistons are of special aluminium alloy with an anodised surface.

The dashboard of the Austin 10 had a Lucas instrument panel. There were two large dials, the right one containing a TPE needle-type speedometer, and the left one containing three smaller dials. These are gauges for the fuel tank, an amp meter and oil pressure. The lighting and ignition switch is located between these two gauges. When you switch on the Austin, the ignition light glows red. If the voltage is too low, this is immediately visible because the light weakens. Other buttons include a starter and choke and, finally, dashboard lighting. The civilian Austin saloon came with a clock and an ashtray in the centre of the dashboard.

Two buttons on the dashboard operate the windscreen wipers. The electric windscreen wiper sets a number of rods in motion for the wipers. The two buttons can be activated separately. The Austin had an open glove compartment on the left. In this reasonably deep box, a hinged arm moved through the glove compartment. There was a push button for the horn in the centre of the steering wheel. The small switch for trafficators is also located above the steering wheel. These emerge from the B-pillar between the doors.

Its compact size and agility allowed it to navigate narrow roads and rough terrain with ease. It had a top speed of around 60 mph (96 km/h) and a range of over 200 miles (320 km).

At the rear the first production Austins had their licence plate beneath the bumper. This was adjusted to a place on the boot lid in the first months after production started.

Brochure showing the interior of the Austin 10 Saloon 1939. (Author's collection)

Austin 10 Saloon front view. This Austin 10 was used by the Bath Admiralty during the Second World War. (Simon Malpass)

Austin 10 Saloon with early specification blackout and without hubcaps. This specific Austin was registered in Westbury-on-Trym before war broke out and then went back to Longbridge to be used as a WD specification vehicle until 1944. It was then issued its 1944 serial number and surpluses in 1946 in Gloucestershire. (Neil Mitchell)

Rear view of the Austin 10 Saloon. (Raymund van Riel)

Austin 10 Saloon motor compartment. (Raymund van Riel)

Austin 10 Saloon dashboard. (Raymund van Riel)

Differences from the 1939 Austins

The Austin 10 was not the only model that was updated in 1939. The Austin 8, 10, and 16 also had the same family appearance. There were a few minor differences between the 8 and 10. For example, the 10 had a rear window in two parts, but the 8 had a one-piece window. There was also a difference in the mudguards. The mudguards of the 8 had a smooth finish, while those of the 10 had decorative edges.

Austin 8 two-door saloon. (Kuine's Military Photography)

Technically, there were also a few differences, such as the 900-cc engine size of the 8 and overall dimensions of the vehicles. The smaller engine of the 8 also led to a shorter engine bay and bonnet.

The 12 and the later 16 were longer and wider vehicles compared with the 10. The longer hood and wider bumper indicate that it was not a 10. Technically, the 12 had a 1,535-cc engine. For the 16, the bumper was further incorporated into the body of the car.

Austin 10 Van

In the original sales brochure, the Austin 10 Van is not mentioned. The manuals after the war cover the Austin 10 Saloon GSI and Van GVI. The Austin Eight was available as a van before and during the war. The van, of course, had the same recognisable alligator hood and front as the other Austin 10s. The door was widened, something that was done with the Austin Tilly (which used the wider door of the Austin 8 Saloon). This is because the van's loading space was not equipped with the extra seats that the Tilly had. The seat in the back of the Austin Tilly was accessed via the front door. The front seat backs had to be folded forward. The extended front door was therefore necessary to give passengers sufficient entry space. The van's loading space was comparable to the Austin Tilly. The metal casing followed the line of the roof and the wheel arches were recessed on the inside.

Austin 10 Van (found in 2023 on www.parking.be).

Military Deployment of the Austin 10 During the Second World War

During the Second World War, the Austin 10 GRQ was deployed in a supporting role in various theatres of war. These vehicles served with distinction under the British Army, providing vital support to ground forces.

British Army units in the Second World War consisted of a hierarchical structure of armies, divisions, brigades, and battalions. In addition, there were more specific units such as Signals, Engineers, Medical Corps, etc. Each brigade had a number of vehicles assigned to it. Among these vehicles would be several passenger cars with two or four seats. There were up to nine two-seat cars and two four-seat cars assigned to an HQ unit. The lower battalions also often had two or more four-seat cars. These were for the use of officers and administrative units. The Austin saloon and Tilly were vehicles that were intended for this role.

For an infantry division of 18,347 officers and men, several vehicles were needed. Around 495 miscellaneous light vehicles and Jeeps were assigned to a division, including the Austin 10 Saloon, used as a staff car. The saloon would probably be used by officers and as a liaison vehicle by the administration platoon. In the Far East, the saloon was also used by the RAF. The military saloon was a civilian saloon with a few modifications. The engine was a 9.99-hp, 1,125-cc side-valve of 29.5 bhp. The car was identical to the 1940 model, the only exception being that the gearbox third motion shaft flange was separate instead of being integral with the shaft.

As hostilities engulfed Europe in the early stages of the Second World War, the Austin 10 Model 1939 GRQ found itself thrust into a variety of roles on the home front. The home front in Britain saw widespread use of small Austin saloons, particularly the Austin 7 and 10 models, for a variety of purposes essential to the war effort. Here's a detailed description of their roles:

- Civil defence and emergency services: small Austin saloons were often employed by civil defence units. They were used as patrol cars by air-raid wardens, fire services, and the Auxiliary Fire Service (AFS). Their compact size made them ideal for navigating narrow city streets, especially in areas affected by bombing raids.
- Government and military use: various government departments and military units utilised Austin saloons for transportation and communication. They served as staff cars for military officers and government officials, as well as liaison vehicles for delivering messages and coordinating activities between different units and locations.
- Home Guard: the Home Guard, a volunteer defence organisation, used Austin saloons for patrolling and logistical support. These cars facilitated the movement of troops and equipment and provided mobile command posts.
- Community support: beyond official capacities, these vehicles also played a crucial role in the community. Volunteers used them to deliver food, medical supplies, and other essentials to households affected by the war, particularly in rural and remote areas where larger vehicles might struggle with access.

Austin 10 Saloon. Note the exhaust at the end under the chassis. (Raymund van Riel)

From patrolling coastal areas in search of enemy infiltrators to dispatch communications, the saloon proved its versatility and reliability time and again. Its compact dimensions and relatively low fuel consumption made it an ideal choice for civilian defence organisations and auxiliary units tasked with guarding strategic installations.

National Fire Service (NFS)

The NFS had an ingenious method of personnel transport, thereby saving petrol. The London Regional HQ used one or more of the forty-seven staff cars for each journey. This was regulated not by importance or otherwise, but by their number.

The types of cars in the motor pool varied from Austin 8 to 28-hp eight-cylinder Railtons and included examples of Buick, Ford, Hillman, Morris, and many other makes. The Austin 10 Saloon would surely be included in this extensive motor pool.

Police

The Austin 10 was one of the most popular saloon cars in the 1940s – not only as a military staff car. In the Isle of Wight Military and Heritage Museum a version of the Austin 10 Saloon is preserved as a police car. The saloon is equipped with the blackouts for the Blitz and has white-painted bumpers and white paint around the mudguards. During the 1940s police cars had a bell attached beside the grille instead of sirens.

4

The Austin 10 Light Utility Truck (GYG)

General Information

The inter-war period witnessed significant advancements in automotive technology, spurred on in part by the demands of military logistics and transportation. Recognising the need for versatile utility vehicles capable of supporting front-line troops, engineers explored various designs tailored to meet the demands of the British War Office.

Wartime photo of an Austin Tilly with a single early blackout headlight. (Tilly Register Archive)

The entire motor industry of Great Britain delivered an enormous performance. The switch from civilian to the war role caused innovation in production. The Austin 10 Saloon retained its appearance, but some adjustments were made for the Austin Tilly. The Tilly was a creative adjustment, which was produced by four different car manufacturers. These light utility trucks, better known as Tillys, were made by Austin Motor Company, Hillman Motor Company, Morris Motors, and the Standard Company. The name Tilly was used by all four companies as an abbreviation of Utility. Each of these vehicles was based on a pre-war civilian saloon chassis and mechanicals.

The Austin Tilly was the most produced of these four brands. It was characterised by a recognisable silhouette, as were the other three marques. The standard front of a civilian saloon was largely retained but the rear was adapted from the B-pillar into a small pick-up. The rear load space was covered by a canvas hood (tilt). A spare wheel was carried on the metal cab roof in front of the hood, secured in place by a wheel clamp ring and split pin. Only the Standard Tilly did not have a metal cab but had a full canvas hood covering the rear up to the windscreen. The Standard's spare wheel was bolted to the tailgate. The simplicity of rear-wheel drive, combined with a large load space, met the War Department's requirements. Due to the pressures of war, the manufacturers saw opportunities to simplify the Tilly models due to wartime shortages. A limited number of upgrades were also introduced, mainly mechanical, but also things like flanges on all four wheels to aid the use of slings to lift them onto trains or ships. However, these adjustments were not sufficient to keep the Tilly's role unchanged during the war. The arrival of the Jeep caused a slight shift. The power of the Jeep showed that the Tillys lacked power on unpaved or cross-country roads and, indeed, traction. However, Tillys did offer more protection against the elements and had a larger payload. The Jeep had a towing eye and could easily tow an American Bantam trailer or a British 10-cwt trailer. Tillys were never officially fitted with towing eyes. The Jeep became more widely available under Lend-Lease, but the Tilly remained a handy run-about vehicle and was as a light load carrier more suitable, and comfortable, than the Car 5-cwt 4x4. A direct comparison of the Jeep and Tilly is hardly fair.

Austin Tilly stands beside a Jeep. (Author's collection)

On 25 February 1944, *Autocar* magazine published an article, 'An Austin in Khaki', by H. S. Linfield. In this article he described driving the Austin Tilly during the war. He thought back on this with pleasure. This vehicle would be ideal after the war for many civilian owners, especially for countryside use.

The Austin Tilly was available from the second half of 1940, with the first production contract (Contract V3887) taken out in March 1940. 1,757 were ordered, probably for around £165 each. A similar type of vehicle would have been 40 to 50 per cent more expensive after the war and then there was a 33.3 per cent purchase tax in addition. This last was caused by the horsepower tax. The Austin 10, in peacetime, was rated at 9.996 hp. Clearly, it had been designed with its bore ratio to the finest limits to keep the engine within the 10 hp class.

The Austin Tilly had its bore enlarged by 3.15 mm, increasing the capacity to 11.02 hp. Although this still had significance for service purposes, the Austin in peacetime did not really need that extra 100 cc; it was added for the heavier load. The performance of the Austin was good, but although the design could certainly use the extra capacity, this was an issue for sales, and the imposed sales tax. If the Austin was to fall into the 11 hp class, it would be unsellable. The cost would probably be around £320, a price tag for a vehicle that would therefore not be marketable. Sales figures would be far from a commercial success.

Features and Specifications

The Austin Tilly had a similar chassis to the Austin 10 Saloon. The difference was that the front cabin was bolted onto the chassis giving it a stronger, unitary construction. The rear load-carrying area had a wooden frame onto which sheet metal panels were attached. The oddest mention in the Maintenance Manual is the fact that the turning circle to the right was almost a foot less than the left: 35 ft 2 in against 36 ft. The saloon had a turning circle of 38 ft.

Austin Tilly cab and tailgate. (Author's collection)

Modifications or Anomalies

During the five-year production run of the Austin Tilly, several adjustments were made, which were probably very logical at that time. However, because information has not always been preserved, it sometimes prompts questions today to which there are no answers. These anomalies or modifications provide topics of conversation for current and future owners of Austins. Minor adjustments were made throughout the war due to a shortage of materials. For instance, Austin Tillys had four small storage boxes in the loading area. These boxes were originally made of wood but later replaced with metal boxes to save on time, costs, and materials.

The Austin 10 Saloon and Tilly had the same bonnet dimensions. The engine compartment was quite spacious and well-organised. Under the windscreen on the bulkhead was a recess for the batteries. In this day and age, a 12-volt battery would easily fit there, but originally two smaller 6-volt batteries were connected together here. Looking from the front, there is a water pump on the left front of the Tilly engine. This is missing from the saloon. On both engines, the petrol pump is located bottom right. This ensures that fuel is pumped from the tank, which hangs behind the rear axle under the car, to the carburettor. This pump is driven by the engine's camshaft. On the manifold, on the right, is the carburettor with an air filter on top. On the Austin Tilly this is a round oil air filter. A layer of oil in the filter ensures that dirt from the air does not enter the fuel system. The saloon has an elongated cylindrical air filter. As the carburettor is on the other side of the car from the driver, an ingenious way had to be found to connect the accelerator pedal. The result is an accelerator pedal with a long crossbar which runs along the firewall. In this way, the movement of the accelerator pedal is brought from the far right to the left. There, a number of short rods connect the carburettor to the pedal.

The well-known Austin logo is attached to the grille. On top of the bonnet is an art deco-style handle to open the bonnet. By simply turning this handle a quarter turn, the bonnet rises a few inches. The 'safety hook' of the bonnet can simply be pushed back to open the bonnet completely. On the right is a rod to secure the bonnet in the open position. The tapered shape of the hood with a rounded front, and the way it opens, is the reason for the 'alligator' hood name.

Motor compartment, Austin Tilly. (Tilly Register Archive)

Batteries in the motor compartment of an Austin Tilly. (Author's collection)

View of the open bonnet, giving it the nickname alligator. (Tilly Register Archive)

Dashboard

The dashboards of the saloon and Tilly were the same. At the beginning of the war, Austin used the dashboard from the civilian saloon. On this dashboard, in the centre section, was a clock and an ashtray. In a manual for the 10, it is clearly visible in the dashboard that a switch was mounted over the left opening, originally for the ashtray. The place for the clock is covered with a plate. Also, photographs of early and later Tillys confirm that later dashboards had the opening for the ashtray replaced by a smooth metal surface.

The four-cylinder side-valve engine is easily started with a starter knob. Starting all Austins is the same. Military Austins had the same starter and light switch, but without a key. Instead of chrome, this starter had white annotations on a black surface. By turning

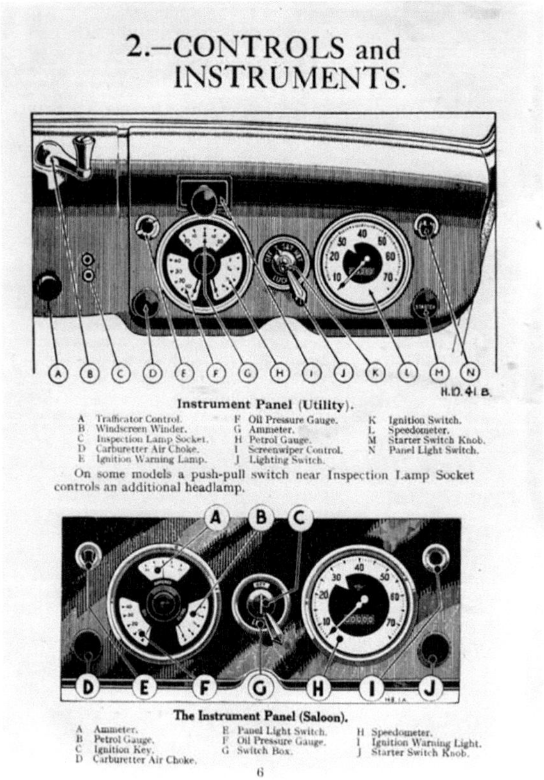

Schematics of the Austin 10 dashboards. (Author's collection)

the switch clockwise, the electrical circuit closed. A light on the dashboard lights up to indicate that power is present. By pulling the starter knob, the starter motor switches on, and the engine starts after a while, because petrol has to be pumped up from the fuel tank. As soon as the oil gauge indicates sufficient pressure – usually between 10 and 20 – the engine starts. Engines from that period still needed a choke for reliable cold starting. As soon as the engine was warm enough to run at idle, the choke was pushed back in. The electric motor for the windscreen wipers was located on the left, against the bulkhead. The wipers were activated via a rod system, concealed behind the dashboard. The manual rotary knobs on the dashboard could be used separately.

Front Seats

From the first contracts, Austin had their original seats covered in Rexine, an imitation leather. How were the seats attached to the floor? On the left of each seat is a notched slider into which simple sprung levers engage (bottom right). The left-side slider is plain. Both sliders have a 'kick-up' at the rear to stop the seat sliding too far rearward. The sliders are attached to the floor with two bolts at the front and one at the rear, picking up on captive nuts in U-shaped strengthening channels under the floorpan. As you can see, these are original unrestored fittings.

Front seats of the Austin Tilly. Also clearly visible is the indicator arm and the pick-axe handle behind the seat. (Tilly Register Archive)

From mid-production Contract 4091-5006, the earlier front seats were replaced by more utilitarian seats with foam bases and backs covered with canvas. The canvas even covered the rear or the seat backs.

The final version of the front seats was very similar to the earlier seats, but the backs of the seats were not covered in canvas, exposing the painted metal-fluted backs.

Rear Seats

The material around the base formed a curtain and hung loose below the seat cushion, partially covering the seat frame. The frame itself is identical to the earlier type. The backs of the seats fold forwards for rear passenger access as per the original seats. For the rear seats, the back and base 'cushions' were made from stretched canvas. The back was a rectangle of canvas screwed to the uprights. The uprights were lined by an arched flat metal bar. The complicated part of the seat was an adjusting system that stretched the bottom canvas when it became loose. The canvas was wrapped around a steel rod that could be tightened by two bolts.

According to the Master Parts List, Austin made three different types of rear seat. The most common and well-known are the folding rear seats with stretched canvas. By folding the seats forward and flat, the loading floor could be enlarged. The backrest folded first allowing the whole seat to tilt forward and flat.

The canvas seat probably came with two types of backrests. In both versions, a strip of canvas was sewn and stretched between the two upper sides of the metal frame. The seat

Rear seats of the Austin Tilly. (Author's collection)

was also made of canvas which was stretched tight by means of two rods. With two adjustment bolts at the back, it could be tightened or loosened.

The third variant is probably the early version and consisted of a wooden seat with a backrest of wood covered with canvas. One surviving example has horsehair as filling. The seat consisted of a wooden subframe with filling, covered with canvas. At the back of the seat were two openings lined with brass ferrules, allowing for some air movement. The seats were handed with different right and left seats (G3-114 and G3-115, respectively). The MPL states that chassis numbers starting 190497 to 209697 used them. Strangely enough, the MPL also lists G3-114.A and G3-115.A used from chassis 209698 to 212674. It is suspected that the production of these early models was too costly and time-consuming.

Trailer

The Austin Tilly was not equipped with a pintle hook. There was some experimentation by the Coldstream Guards with the Mathews Trailer in 1942. This was a small single-axle light-weight trailer with internal wheel arches. The special thing about this trailer was that it did not have a standard towing eye but was attached to the towing vehicle with a metal beam, usually to the bumper mounting points. Two drawbars ran from the trailer to the

Austin Tilly with a Mathews trailer. (IWM H 21713, IWM)

beam, so that it was connected to the towing vehicle at two points. The two rods could extend and retract when the vehicle made a bend by using a spring construction. These trailers were not used in service.

Headlights

Listed in the first Austin parts list for Contract V3887 was a saloon-type headlamp, Lucas MD143, fitted from the side on the ends of a mounting tube through both bonnet sides (with the cable neatly fed through it). Apparently, in this contract, twin headlamps were fitted. Photos of this installation are very rare. The only known image is on what is believed to be the prototype Austin Tilly. Later, during Contract V3887, a revised headlamp was introduced, the Lucas MD140, still in pairs. These were mounted above the bar on the left-hand side only. It was here that, for the first time, the cable was fed through a grommet-protected hole in the bodywork below the mounting tube. From V4065, only a single was mounted on the left-hand side.

From mid-Contract V4374, the third and final type of headlamp was introduced in 1941. This was the single standard Lucas L-WD-H1, along with the Butler variant, the B-WD-H1, which was produced in huge numbers and used on a vast number of vehicles. Although the Butler version is never mentioned in the parts lists, this headlight must have been fitted to Austin Tillys as there are far too many surviving vehicles, many untouched for a very long time, that use them. This headlight had a blackout mask and was mounted only on the left side.

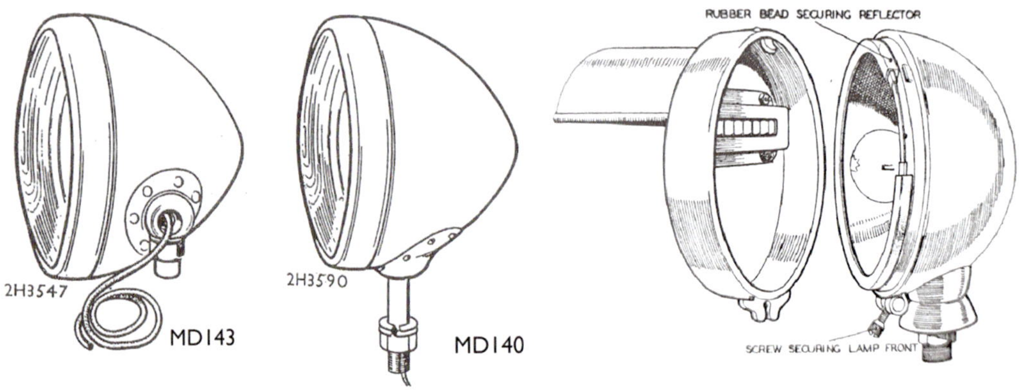

Three different headlights of the Austin Tilly. (Author's collection)

Tail Light

The first Tillys had two central lights fitted – tail and stop lamps – hence the shape of the hole at the tailgate. A single central light became common from V4091 in August 1940. Also, of note here is that the rear bumper had angled ends, which are not noted in the production tables.

Tailgate

The pressed-steel tailgate was introduced in Contract V4065 in June 1940. Early tilts had the square cut-outs for the tailgate pegs, later deleted in the quest for simplification.

The Austin Tilly metal tailgate. Note the double tail lights. (Author's collection)

Austin is supposed to have a pressed-steel tailgate. Sometimes you can see an Austin with a wooden tailgate, but that is a post-war tailgate. This is because a steel tailgate was not available and a wooden tailgate was cheaper to make.

Toolboxes

The Austin Tilly has four separate toolboxes in the load compartment. These are located on the sides, in front of and behind the wheel arches. On the rear left, the hose for the fuel filler cap to the fuel tank runs through the toolbox. On the same side, the front toolbox has a compartment under the lid for storing a driver's handbook or other manual. Originally, toolbox lids were made of wood. Later toolboxes had metal lids.

Left side of the cargo area showing the boxes with wooden lids. (Author's collection)

Boxes with metal lids. (Tilly Register Archive)

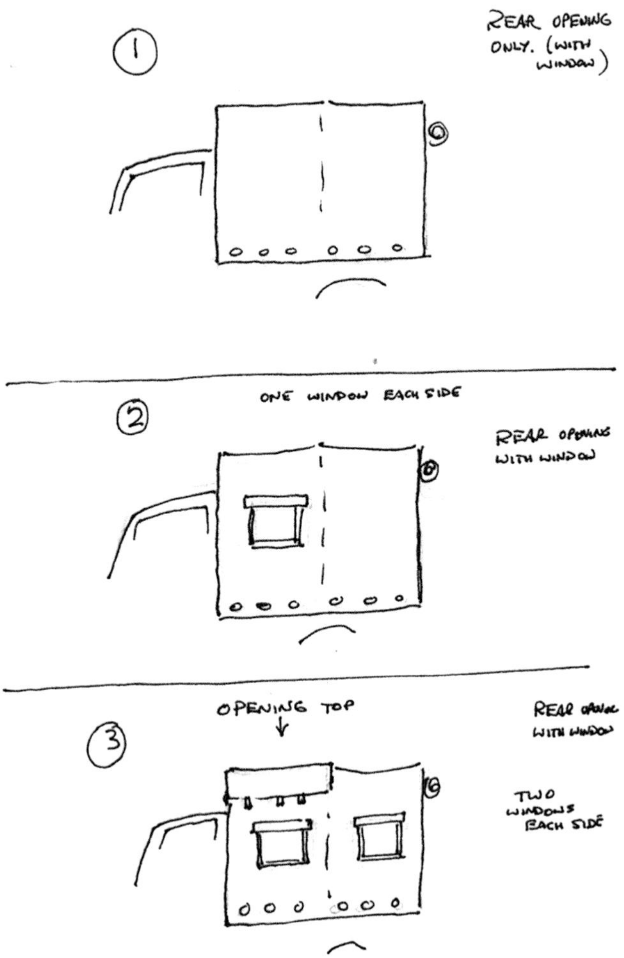

Schematic of tilts. (Tilly Register Archive)

Tilt

Different sorts of tilts or canopy were supplied for the Austin Tilly. This was simplified as the war progressed. Each canopy had its own features. The original was the most complex, with two windows each side and another in the rear. The window openings were covered in a very fine mesh, not clear plastic. The front part of the top could be folded back, creating an opening. A soldier with a Bren gun gave limited local defence (not necessarily air defence as the bipod restricted enough elevation of the gun) while standing in the opening. He did this by resting the Bren gun's bipod on the spare wheel. The second style of tilt did away with the rearmost windows on the sides but retained the opening top. There doesn't seem to be any logic as to when these variations were introduced. The final style of tilt did away with the two remaining side windows and the opening top, just keeping a single window in the opening rear panel. The canopy was made until at least until 1949. This suggests that Austin Tillys were used for some years after the war by the military.

Austin Tilly with early tilt with flap on front. This Tilly also has the brake light and a tail light at the rear before the brake light was deleted during Contract V4374 of December 1940. (Tilly Register Archive)

Austin Tilly with one-piece tilt with side window. (Tilly Register Archive)

In another Tilly make, the Hillman, it was possible to mount a Motley mount for local defence in the cargo space. The Motley mount was a tube construction, with a rotating chair and mounts for one or two Bren guns. This meant that the gunner did not have to continuously carry the weight of the Bren guns himself. The chair could rotate 360 degrees but would have had only a limited range for air defence. It is not known whether this was ever installed in an Austin Tilly. The tilt would have been removed altogether to use this equipment. There is no confirmation that the Motley was ever used in the Austin.

Austin Tilly with tilt in one piece. (Author's collection)

Austin Tilly at Normandy beach without a tilt. (Tilly Register Archive)

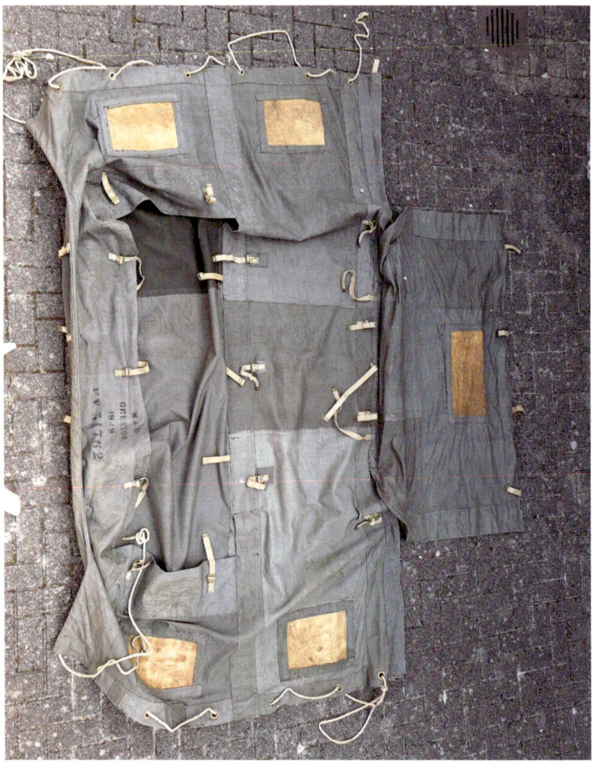

A tilt from 1949 showing all the straps to secure it to the Austin. (Author's collection)

Split Cabin

Part way through Contract V5015 a split cab was introduced. This adjustment for the cabin was devised in 1942 for the transportation of the Austin Tilly. The idea was that a divisible (split) cab would be helpful in transporting the car. A divisible cabin lowered the profile of the vehicle and thus took up less space. However, it is unclear whether it was actually used. Photographs of loading an Austin Tilly onto a ship show the vehicle with the cab in one piece. Several surviving Austins have such split cabs. The unbolting points were located on the windscreen pillars (the screen itself, and doors, would be removed) and there were bolted brackets on the headboard dividing the cab from the load area.

The height of the normal Tilly was 6 ft 2.5 in. The cut-down height for shipment was, according to the last contract, 5 ft 5.75 in.

Differences Between the Saloon and Tilly

Today's preserved examples of Tillys are almost entirely in private hands. Very limited numbers are in museum collections, with only one Hillman and Standard coming to mind. Owners display their vehicles at meetings, commemorations, and rallies. In the past, the vehicles were overlooked, even by military vehicle enthusiasts. Nowadays, although still outnumbered by Jeeps and Dodges (at least in mainland UK or Europe), you can find them at some military shows. However, this special little vehicle now gets more attention from military vehicle owners and the general public.

The Austin Tilly was based on the 10 Saloon but is different in several respects. The Morris and Hillman Tilly are similar vehicles. Just like the Austin, they are all based on their civilian saloon equivalents, but with an important difference. The Hillman and Morris have doors that are the same as their equivalent saloon cars. However, the Austin Tilly has doors that are larger. In fact, the doors are 10 inches wider and are the same as the two-door Austin 10. The wider door is one of the many differences between the civilian Austin 10 Saloon and Tilly. Not surprisingly, a number of differences are shared with the military

Austin 10 Saloon and Tilly waiting to start the Liberation Task Force event at Leopoldsburg, Belgium, in 2024.

saloon. The main differences between the saloon and Tilly are the grille, doors, engine, dashboard, seats, rear part of the chassis, and electrical system. The difference between the grilles is that it had solid pressed slats which, of course, were not chrome plated. At some point during the war, the number of slats was reduced to simplify production.

Both vehicles had a four-cylinder side-valve engine, but the Tilly's engine had a larger displacement, as mentioned above.

The dashboard of both Austins were almost the same. The main switch of a civilian saloon is chrome-plated and has an ignition lock with key. For military use, the main switch was replaced by the military black Bakelite switch. This switch was standard for many military vehicles.

The saloon has two chairs with a wooden base frame. The leather seat is equipped with springs and the backrest is also equipped with springs. The Tilly has two front seats in the form of metal bucket seats. These chairs are placed on the floor with metal guides. The saloon has slightly wider seats and these are placed on wooden blocks with guides on the floor.

The fuel tank of the Tilly has a slightly larger capacity, from 8.5 gallons against 6 gallons for the saloon.

Finally, the electrical system of the military Austin Tilly was negative earth, unlike the saloon car. As a result, electrical parts, such as alternators, are not interchangeable between the Tilly and the civilian saloon. The military saloon retained the electrical system from the civilian vehicle. That is to say it was positively grounded, unlike the Tillys.

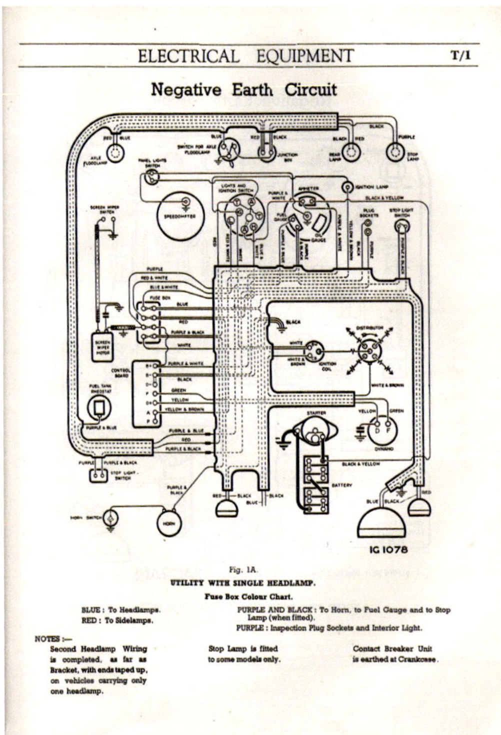

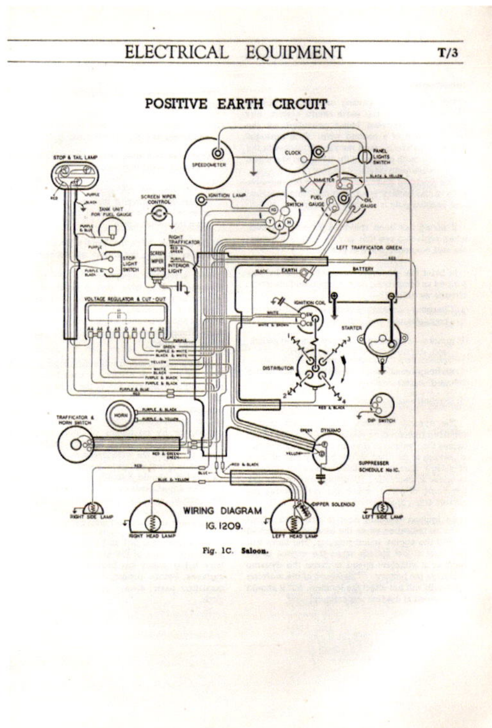

Electrical systems for Austin saloon and Tilly. (Author's collection)

Military Deployment During Wartime Operations

The Second World War was characterised by fast movement of the motorised army. The capacity to move quickly had been given to modern armies by the motor vehicle, not, as many suppose, by tanks and other armoured fighting vehicles. Where would the tank and armoured car be without support from infantry and artillery? Alongside larger lorries, the small Tillys fulfilled an important role. In photographs from many theatres of the war, Tillys can be found somewhere in the second line: from the early stages in France, to the Battle of Britain, the North African campaign and into Italy and the Balkans, from the D-Day landings in Normandy to the liberation of the Netherlands and Germany. A Tilly was there to fulfil its light logistic role.

Austin and Hillman Tillys at a military garage. (Tilly Register Archive)

Austin Tilly during a parade in The Hague in 1945. The Austin was used by the Dutch Princess Irene Brigade. Some civilians mounted the vehicles during the parade. (Tilly Register Archive)

Even in the British Expeditionary Force, the contingent of the British Army that was sent to France in 1939, Austins were present.

As the demands of modern warfare evolved, so too did the role of the Tilly. The design of the Austin Tilly with its load space and seats that could be folded down made the Austin Tilly a multi-purpose vehicle. Specialised variants were equipped for tasks such as field ambulance service, signal relay, and transport for commanding officers. In addition to their logistical functions, the saloon and Tilly played crucial roles in supporting troop movements and tactical operations by supplying troops with the necessary equipment, ammunition, food, spares, etc.

Medical and Rescue Operations

Perhaps most importantly, the saloon and Tilly served as lifelines for wounded soldiers on the battlefield, providing timely evacuation and medical care under the most challenging conditions. Equipped as field ambulances or fitted with twin stretchers (in the Tilly) for casualty transport, these vehicles played a critical part in the chain of evacuation, ensuring that injured personnel received the care they desperately needed. In this way, GRQ and Tilly contributed to the overall effectiveness of Allied medical services to front-line troops.

Home Guard

Various vehicles were also used by the Home Guard. Whether the Home Guard also used the Austin Tilly has not been confirmed, but the likelihood that they used Austin saloons and other civilian vehicles is high. Sometimes these were older civilian trucks and cars. The Austin 10 Saloon, and also saloons of other brands, were generally not painted in army colours. They retained their original colour, but it was customary to provide vehicles with white elements. Parts of the bumpers were painted white and an edge around the mudguards was also added. These white markings were intended to provide

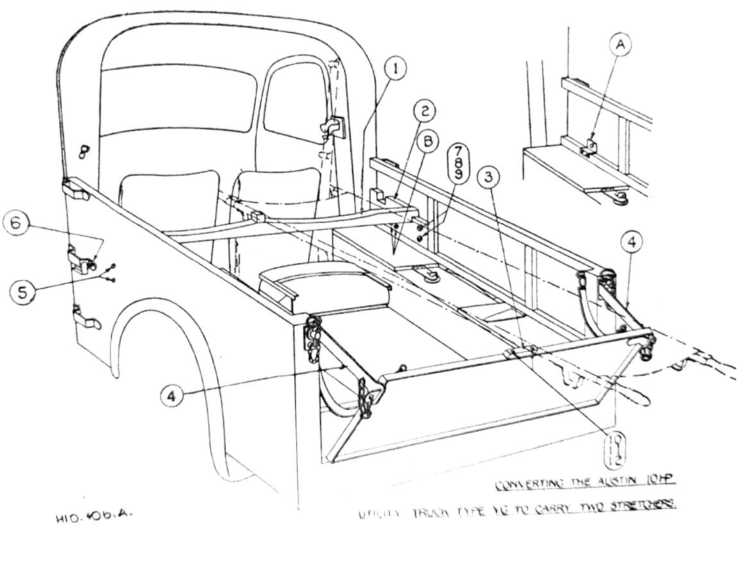

Schematic from the Austin Tilly maintenance manual for the placement of stretchers in the rear. (Author's collection)

some visibility in the dark during the blackout. The headlights were also equipped with a blackout lamp.

Land Army

The Women's Land Army (WLA) made a significant contribution to boosting Britain's food production during the Second World War. Before the war, Britain imported much of its food. When war broke out, it was necessary to grow more food at home and increase the amount of cultivated land. With many male agricultural workers joining the armed forces, women were needed to provide a new rural workforce.

The WLA had originally been set up in 1917 but was disbanded at the end of the First World War, reforming in June 1939. Women were initially asked to volunteer to serve in the Land Army and, from December 1941, could also be conscripted into land work. At its peak in 1944, there were more than 80,000 women – often known as 'land girls' – in the WLA. Land girls did a wide variety of jobs on the land. They worked in all weathers and conditions and could be directed to work anywhere in the country. It is said that the Land Army also used the Austin Tilly.

Bomb Disposal

In 1939 the War Office decided that the Royal Engineers would provide temporary bomb disposal teams until the Home Office recruited and trained special ARP (Air Raid Precaution) teams to do so. These teams were deployed to dismantle or safely remove unexploded bombs. The Formation Order of May 1940 formally handed responsibility for bomb disposal to the Royal Engineers and created twenty-five bomb disposal sections, soon increasing to 134. In 1942 and 1944, BD Companies also joined the task forces for the invasions of Italy and France. Peace in 1945 resulted in a drastic reduction of BD units along with the rest of the army, and by January 1950 RE BD consisted of one regular squadron headquartered in London and six independent territorial squadrons, later reformed into Army Emergency Reserve Squadrons. These special teams used the Tilly. In order to make the function of this team clear from afar, the vehicles were painted in a specific way. The base was the standard army green colour, but the mudguards were painted bright red. Beside Tillys, the bomb disposal teams also used a variation of saloons.

Austins in the ATS

The Auxiliary Territorial Service (ATS) was the women's branch of the British Army during the Second World War. It was formed on 9 September 1938, initially as a women's voluntary service, and existed until 1 February 1949, when it became part of the Women's Royal Army Corps. As more men joined the war effort, it was decided to increase the size of the ATS, with numbers reaching 65,000 by September 1941. Women between the ages of 17 and 43 were permitted to join, although these rules were relaxed in order to allow WAAC veterans to join up to the age of 50. Members' roles were also expanded and included ATS orderlies, drivers, postal workers and ammunition inspectors.

An ATS Vehicle Maintenance class, with Princess Elizabeth in overalls and cap looking on from the right. (IWM H 41643, IWM)

Famous members of the ATS included Mary Churchill, youngest daughter of Prime Minister Winston Churchill, and Princess Elizabeth, later Queen Elizabeth II, the eldest daughter of the king, who trained as a lorry driver, ambulance driver, and mechanic.

Religious Use

The light utility trucks were multi-functional vehicles. The size and the loading area made them suitable for religious purposes and tending to men in the field in need of spiritual guidance. Padres could easily hold Mass for troops using the small truck. By folding down the tailgate, padres could create a small altar.

Inspections of Troops and Parades

Every army unit has a hierarchical structure, but the general does not give direct leadership to the soldiers. The chain of command ensures the transfer of orders. At certain times it

Using the tailboard of his 'Utility' as his altar, Father C. V. Murphy offers Mass in a Dutch field on the front line. Photograph taken by Sergeant Mapham, 6 October 1944. (IWM B10583, IWM)

Austin Tilly used as a grandstand by His Majesty King George VI, Major General D. C. Bullen-Smith, MC, and Divisional GOC and Lieutenant Colonel J. E. G. Day, OC 5/7 Gordon Highlanders, Vache Camp. (IWM H36232, IWM)

is, of course, good for morale that the high command inspects troops in the field. For this, the Austin Tilly proved to be a suitable vehicle. A Tilly was used several times to help generals, field marshals, and even the king to inspect the troops and units.

Manuals and Contracts

Contracts

For each batch of vehicles, the War Department gave separate orders to the various car manufacturers. The War Department did not simply order in large numbers like 30,000 units but ordered in smaller numbers in separate contracts during the period from 1939 to 1945. The largest order was Contract S1444 of 23 October 1942, for 5,250 units of the Austin Light Utility. Originally, this was an order for 6,000 vehicles. Due to the various contracts, it was possible for the Austin Motor Company to make changes to the Tilly. In general, these were only details and mostly not visible from the outside. It even happened that, within a contract, adjustments were made to the vehicle. The table in Appendix B below gives an indication of the contracts, vehicles, and possible adjustments. It is thanks to this overview that an Austin Tilly can be traced back to the year of manufacture and contract number by just the chassis number. Unfortunately, complete contract information is not available as it has been lost over the years. However, a very good estimate can be made of the VRN (vehicle registration number) that was on the bonnet at the time.

Austin 10 numbering started back in 1932 with 101 for the first Austin 10. This numbering followed for all models of the 10 which ended in October 1947 with 282764. That was the moment that the production of the Austin 10 stopped after a period of around fifteen years. The prefix, such as GRQ, indicated the body type. The GYG Light Utility Truck chassis numbers ran from 19049 to approximately 228650. Because the Tilly was not the only Austin 10 produced in the period 1939–45, a number of the intermediate serial numbers are for the GRQ and, from 1944, for the GSI.

However, there are also parts lists from June 1946 which again mention Austin 10 (GRQ). This manual (publication Number 211A) provides information from May 1939 to July 1945 with Austin GRQ chassis numbers 177362 to 226800 produced by Austin Motor Co. Ltd. This means that approximately 49,000 Austin 10s were produced in this period. A large number included in these chassis numbers were Austin Light Utilities. Production of the Austin Tilly ended with approximately 29,000 having been built.

Other chassis numbers – 223201 to 223206 and 225001 to 226794 – were delivered, according to a spare parts list from the end of 1944. A striking detail is that a note has been made for chassis number 226273, with a prefix of GSI.

According to these figures, approximately 55,000 saloons (GSI) and vans (GVI) were made after the war. This is significantly higher than the original GRQ. The van was the delivery version, actually an enclosed Tilly.

In 1939, production of the new Austin saloon started. Besides the GRQ Saloon and GQC Tourer, the GVE Van was also produced. In 1941, the GRQ Saloon was fitted with a new gearbox with the Third Motion Shaft – from chassis number 192101 onwards. In 1944, production of the GRQ Saloon ended, and the GSI Saloon was produced from chassis number 225718. In July 1945, the production of the GSI Saloon continued with chassis number 226074. This saloon was fitted with a rear axle with a 7.38 ratio (instead of 8.43) and a 'cam gear' steering box. The GVI Van was fitted with a 1,237-cc engine from chassis number 226805, after 1945. The Saloon GSI toolbox was different and included a Stephenson jack (instead of the Midas or Shelly jack). In October 1947, production of the Austin 10 ended with chassis number 282764.

Unfortunately, during the Second World War, there were many contracts for Car, two-seater 4x2. Both the Austin Tilly and Austin 8AP Military Tourer were designated as two-seaters. The Austin GRQ Maintenance Manual states four-seater, not Austin 10 Saloon, because it had a spacious rear seat and therefore four seats. In the past, all contract numbers from different manufacturers were noted in the 'Allocation by Central census "B" vehicle W.D. numbers'. This book by Rob van Meel was compiled based on a publication by the Royal Army Ordnance Corps Central Ordnance Depot at Chilwell.

Only a few contracts in Rob van Meel's book are directly assigned to the military Saloon GRQ. These possible contracts are mentioned in Appendix B.

For a number of reasons, such as typographical errors in original sources, but also possible errors in processing and contradictory sources, the allocation is not perfect. However, it does give a fairly good estimate that at least 10,000 military Austin 10 Saloons were ordered by the War Department.

Manuals

It was common for automobile manufacturers to supply multiple manuals with a vehicle. In general, a vehicle was supplied with a Driver's Manual, a Spare Parts List, and a Maintenance Manual. Sometimes a fourth manual, or Handbook of the vehicle, was supplied. All manuals had their own individual publication numbers (and dates and War Office contract numbers).

Maintenance Manual with publication number 101/AN3A was for the Austin Utility Truck. Publication 101/AN3B combined the information for the Austin two-seater 4x2 Light Utility and for the four-seater 4x2 Saloon.

Military manuals for the Austin vehicles had red lettering on the front instead of the standard black. Occasionally it was also mentioned which chassis numbers the manual was for. In addition to a publication number, the corresponding military contract number was also mentioned.

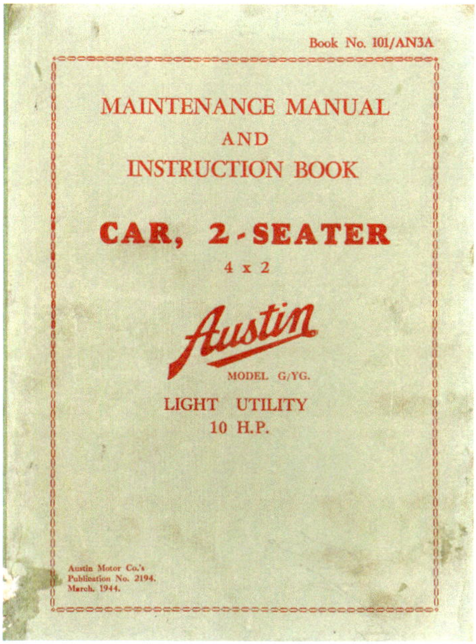

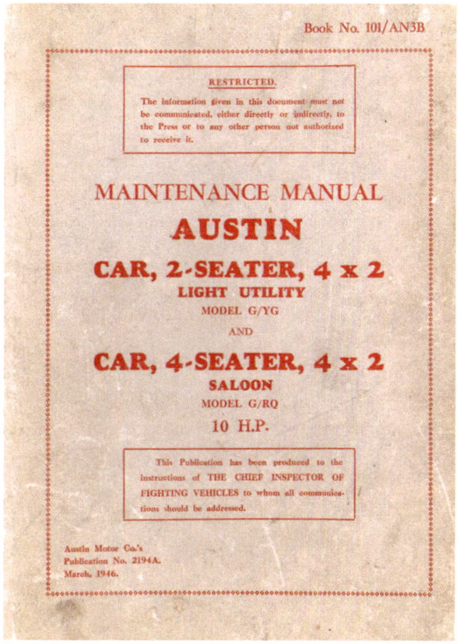

Austin Maintenance Manuals for Tilly and combined for both vehicles. (Author's collection)

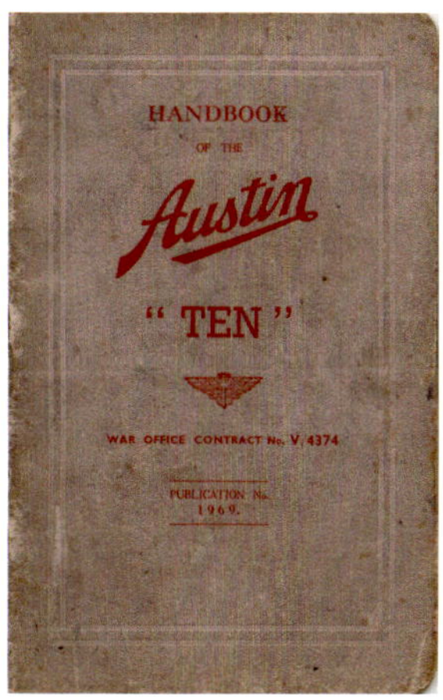

Austin Tilly manuals. (Author's collection)

Questionnaire and Manuals

The various Austin vehicles, such as the 3-ton 4x4 GS, Portee and Austin Car Light Utility 4x2, remained in service after the war. This also meant that maintenance had to be carried out on the vehicles.

Of course, the various manuals for the vehicles were available, but the Army Mechanical Transport Service (AMTS) prepared a questionnaire for fast service and troubleshooting for these vehicles. In the questionnaire of February 1946, all kinds of technical questions were answered. These covered topics such as what kind of oil and what capacity, but also where the oil filter was located and how to replace it. The questionnaire also included very useful fault-finding tables.

In addition to the various technical questions, these questionnaires contained a summary of various Directorate of Mechanical Engineering (DME) circulars. These circulars had an effect on vehicles of this type and make.

Circular 49 of 4 December 1940 prescribed the fitting of an extra rear light on Tillys and cars such as the saloon.

Circular 308 of 22 December 1943 is particularly interesting. This prescribed that two stretchers had to be fitted in the Tilly. In some preserved Austin Tillys, this modification is still visible. On the body sides of the load area, at the height of the folding seats, two wooden blocks were fixed. A crossbeam spanned the loading space. The two stretchers were then supported at the rear on the tailgate (with a spacer in the centre). The medic then sat in the front. Circular B512 of 24 June 1943 featured a silencer and tailpipe assembly for Tillys.

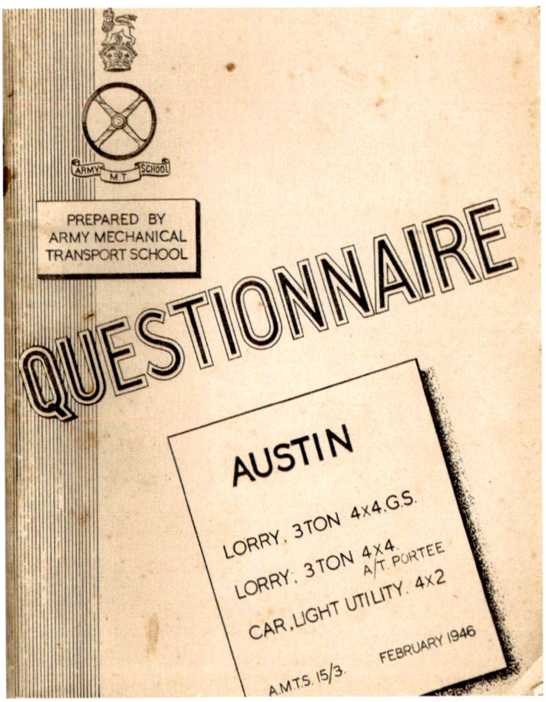

This questionnaire was used by the Army Mechanical Transport School to train mechanics. (Author's collection)

Colour and Camouflage Patterns

During the Second World War, British AFV and vehicle camouflage was determined by a number of Army Council Instructions (ACIs) and Military Training Pamphlets (MTPs). Colours used were supplied pre-mixed, matching two British Standards – BS.381C of 1930 and BS.987C of 1942 – together with some non-standard paints for specific purposes.

Europe

Up until 1939, an overall gloss colour of Deep Bronze Green No. 24 was the usual finish, applied in the factory, for all vehicles. In photographs this often appears as almost black.

In 1939–41 bold horizontal/diagonal patterns of two greens were used following MTP 20 of June 1939. The most usual colours were a basic of Khaki Green No. 3 and Dark Green No. 4. Plain G3 was an occasional alternative. Some vehicles were only overall Khaki Green No. 3 and occasionally Light Green G5 as a disrupter in lieu of Dark Green G4.

Several saloons being camouflaged at a car park while an Austin Tilly arrives. (IWM H16321, IWM)

Austin Tilly in early camouflage pattern. (Tilly Register Archive)

Austin Tilly in green colour. (Kuine's Military Photography)

In January 1941, a variation of colour took place with ACI 1559. Wood and metal bodywork was painted Khaki Green No. 3 and Dark Green G4 with canvas hoods and tilts in SCC 7 and SCC 1A to the same pattern as MTP 20, resulting in a green/black-grey and green/brown scheme.

In 1941–42 Standard Camouflage Colour shades (SCC) from BS.987C came into use alongside (and then replacing the greens), but in the same MTP patterns. The basic shade was Khaki Green No. 3 or SCC 2 Brown, with SCC 1A over it. These browns were introduced as a result of a severe shortage of a vital chemical agent used to produce strong greens.

In 1942–44 MTP 46/4A introduced new toned schemes aimed primarily against aerial observation, usually featuring the BS.987C browns. The most common versions were variants of the 'Foliage' pattern and the 'Mickey Mouse' variant of the 'Dapple' pattern. Vehicles continued to be delivered and used in plain SCC 2 Brown. In October 1943, SCC 14 Black was authorised as the main shade over SCC 2 Brown.

The final change in colouring came in April 1944 when SCC 15 Olive Drab was used as the new basic colour, partially to remove the need to repaint American-supplied vehicles. SCC 15 Olive Drab was used to cover the obsolete SCC 2 Brown in MTP 46/4A patterns or on its own, particularly after the abandonment of disruptive painting from August 1944, except on vehicles still in SCC 2 Brown.

In Italy, vehicles used Home Forces schemes as outlined above. Softskin vehicles were the basic colour inside.

Also specific to softskins:

> Pre-war until 1941 Tilts were a light canvas colour, in 1940–41 painted over with MTP 20 bands in the darker colour used – usually G3. Tilts could also be dyed Khaki Green No. 3 over which G4 might be painted.

In August 1941 Khaki Green No. 3 and Dark Green G4 (the RAF designation was Nobel's Dark Tarmac Green No. 4) was used on bodywork with bituminous emulsion of SCC 7 and SCC 1A (dark brown) on canvas surfaces.

Austin Tilly in Mickey Mouse camouflage. (Kuine's Military Photography)

From November 1941, with MTP 20 still specified, all top horizontal surfaces were to be SCC 1A or, if unavailable, SCC 14 (black). SCC 2 Brown was used to restore faded tilts. New tilts and hoods were now manufactured from canvas dyed to a near match for SCC 2 Brown.

In August 1944, Tilts were dyed SCC 15 Olive Drab rather than SCC 2 Brown. Bituminous Emulsion SCC 7 (green) could be used on tents, penthouses, and hoods where SCC 15 was not available.

Middle East

As far as Tillys and other second-line vehicles were concerned, they retained the colour schemes they used when they were shipped to theatre from the UK. Malta (also see below) was the exception where they adopted a distinctive design generally known as 'stone wall', a series of light-coloured blocks with a darker colour as 'shadow' lines. This scheme varied immensely from the neat appearance of stonework through crazy paving to straight lines similar to a chessboard. The colours varied from Khaki Green No. 3 lines with Light Stone No. 61 or Portland Stone No. 64 'stones' over it, to darker lines painted over the original sand colour depending on country of origin.

RAF Colours, 1939–45

At the outbreak of war in 1939, RAF vehicles were painted in peacetime BS 33 RAF Blue/Grey. In 1940, when the Battle of Britain brought aerial warfare to the British Isles, it was considered that camouflage was needed. Many vehicles were painted in the Dark Earth and Dark Green colours of aircraft or the building camouflage colours of brown and green.

It was not until 1941 that a directive on overall standard camouflage for RAF MT vehicles was issued. RAF (and navy) colours echoed army orders. This order covered all vehicles including those pressed into RAF service, but excluded vehicles used by officers of Air Commodore rank and above.

As gas attacks were expected throughout the war, a 6-inch by 6-inch patch of gas detector paint was painted, visible to the driver from the cab. In 1943, it was decided that gas detector paint would be introduced to cover all vehicles then in production, the new colours being MT Brown Special SCC 2 and Quick Drying Black SCC 14, the idea being that vehicles parked near buildings on airfields would contrast with the shadow of the buildings, especially in winter.

In the run-up to summer 1944, all vehicles would have been painted Olive Drab in place of the brown, the black remaining. In September 1944, Olive Drab was adopted as the overall camouflage colour and black patterning was discontinued. This held good until 1946 when peacetime schemes were reintroduced, and Olive Drab gave way to semi-gloss Blue/Grey. Vehicles in the production stage were painted in the new colours before leaving the factory and others were changed when re-painting was due. Even when Olive Drab was 'in', some factories were still using up their old stock of MT Special Brown.

The Famous Maltese Pattern

One of the most distinctive camouflage patterns was the Maltese stone wall scheme. When vehicles arrived in Malta, they were initially painted in the same camouflage used in Britain. A base coat of sand colour was applied to prevent them from standing out as military vehicles. The Malta camouflage scheme is said to have originated with two soldiers who had received a disciplinary measure for a minor military offence. A sergeant

Austin Tilly getting an invasion star on the bonnet. (IWM H38818, IWM)

instructed them to 'make that vehicle disappear'. Unfortunately for the sergeant, one of the soldiers was a graphic artist. He grabbed a paintbrush and some brown paint, transforming the sand-coloured vehicle to resemble the typical Maltese dry-stone wall it had been parked next to. When the sergeant returned, he was furious, but a passing officer noticed that the paint scheme actually worked. It disrupted the vehicle's outline and helped it blend into the local environment. The paint scheme does not appear in any official army documents, nor is there an official RAL paint number for the sand colour. The paint was mixed and blended by the Maltese soldiers assigned to paint the vehicles. As a result, each of the surviving Malta Austin Tillys features a different shade of sand paint – some have brown lines, while others have black lines. The variation depended on the 'as delivered from Britain' camouflage colours.

Austin Tilly in Maltese pattern. (Tilly Register Archive)

5

The Post-war Austin 10

Transition to Peacetime Production

With the conclusion of the Second World War, the Austin Motor Company faced the challenge of transitioning from wartime to peacetime manufacturing. Despite the significant disruptions caused by the conflict, the company quickly adapted its facilities to resume the production of civilian vehicles. This included the Austin 10 Saloon.

The 1939 design of the saloon was not changed during the war. As production for the civilian market started again, small changes were adopted. Only when two models from different production years are alongside can the differences be detected by the trained eye.

Pre-war, the bumpers and over-riders had rubber mounted on them. Probably because of shortages of rubber post-war, the later model had fully chromed bumpers and over-riders, without rubber fitted.

The post-war saloon had the licence plate holder fitted with tail lights at each side. The 1939 saloon had one tail light above the licence plate in the centre.

The interior didn't change much. The leather seats and back couch were stitched in the same manner and the way they were fitted also did not change. The only visible difference in the interior of the saloon is that after the war an armrest was integrated into the backrest of the rear seat.

The van reappeared post-war with a slightly larger 1,237-cc engine.

Due to the post-war financial crisis, the cars were nearly all exported, with the first one arriving in the United States in July 1945. In September 1945, the first passenger cars produced after the war were sent to Switzerland where two Austin 10s arrived from England. The Austin 10 continued in production in saloon and van form until October 1947. The Austin A40 replaced it.

Post-war Use in the Army After 1945

Thanks to photographic material, it is known that the Austin Tilly served in several armies after the Second World War. A number of countries that had independent units during the

Post-war use of an Austin Tilly in the Danish Army. (Tilly Register Archive)

war, such as the Dutch Princess Irene Brigade, already used Tillys in the war. The number of Austin Tillys serving abroad was low, so foreign service is not well documented. Besides Great Britain, Austin Tillys were used by Belgium, Denmark, Greece, the Netherlands, Portugal, and Sweden.

In 2005 two Austin Tillys turned up in Belgium. Both were complete, and one still had the wooden blocks for the stretcher in the side panels. The markings on the mudguards were from the Belgium Army.

Rebuilds

Within the British Army it was common practice for in-service military vehicles to be rebuilt. This also applied to the Austin Tilly. The vehicles were then considered new and used as such. During the rebuild new (new old stock) parts were used, but sometimes parts were reused from another existing vehicle. The latter was then a donor for multiple rebuilds.

A well-known WD contractor was Weybridge Automobiles, who specialised in Austins. From 1947, all vehicles in British Army service were renumbered, with the previous VRNs being replaced by a two-digit, two-letter, two-digit system, examples of which are 86RB61, 00RC83, 91RD81, and 02RG05.

Special data plates from the Ministry of Supply were placed beside the original chassis number on the engine bulkhead. For example, the Austin with chassis number 194873 became 00RA23 after its rebuild in June 1949. This particular Austin was also overhauled in May 1952. It was shipped to Malta and sold into civilian use until it could no longer be used.

Rebuild plate gives more information about the history and maintenance of a vehicle. (Tilly Register Archive)

Civilian Applications and Economic Recovery

In the years following the Second World War, the Austin 10 Model 1939 GRQ and Tilly found new roles in civilian life. They served as versatile platforms for a wide range of commercial and recreational activities. From agricultural work to urban delivery services, these vehicles proved their worth in countless applications, contributing to the economic recovery and reconstruction efforts of war-torn nations. Moreover, their rugged construction and dependable performance endeared them to generations of motorists seeking practical, affordable transportation options.

Other Austins were bought at army disposal auctions. These vehicles became, like other former military vehicles such as Bedfords and CMPs (Canadian Military Pattern), the backbone of the economy that had to be built up after the war in Europe. These vehicles had a hard life and most of them were used to the maximum. Only a few of these workhorses survived. Most of them can still be found in Malta.

It was not uncommon to replace the engine and gearbox for better performance and thus extend the vehicle's lifespan. Traces of the Austin Tillys being used in other parts of Europe are difficult to find, but there are a few photos of Austin Tillys in civilian use in the Netherlands. The chance of finding an Austin with civilian use is slim, but in 2013 two Austin Tillys turned up in Portugal. Despite their long life they were still in good enough condition for restoration by a willing private owner.

It is difficult to say how many Austins made it to mainland Europe. While not many photographs exist to prove this, there is evidence that they were used for all kinds of purposes besides the military. The small cargo space of the Austin Tilly made it perfect for small loads for small entrepreneurs. However, many Austins were probably scrapped at the end of their lifecycle, as with any car.

In the UK, the Austin Tillys were retired from the British Army in the 1950s. The vehicles were bought in the UK and Europe by all sorts of individuals, varying from farmers to local shopkeepers, from shoe salesmen to those running food businesses. Large numbers were shipped and auctioned in Malta where many still survive, though none are now in use on a daily basis.

Austin Tilly in post-war use by a shoe merchant in the Netherlands. The Austin is decorated with ribbons to celebrate the liberation. (Historisch's-Gravendeel)

Austin Tilly used by a farmer in Malta. (Tilly Register Archive)

Restored Austin in civilian bright blue in Malta. (Tilly Register Archive)

Austin Tilly in bomb disposal colours. (Tilly Register Archive)

On Malta, some Austin Tillys had very bright and decorative colour schemes with advertising on the doors, bonnet or on the tilt. Names and addresses of businesses were proudly displayed. The engine was often replaced, immediately or later by a more modern, more powerful, or more economical engine. Austin Devon, Austin Cambridge, Morris Minor 1000, Morris Marina, or even diesels are all examples of different engines used in Maltese Tillys. The gearbox was also often replaced. A different engine block meant several structural adjustments to the floor and bulkhead and extra mounting points for the engine and gearbox. In some cases, more cooling had to be arranged. This was done by adjusting the side panels with extra openings. Also, the lighting of the tube-mounted headlamps was sometimes moved to a place on, or even in, the mudguards. In the 1960s, there was a known example of an Austin being bought from a local garage. The cost of the Austin at that time was £10, even with several post-war modifications.

Legacy

The Austin 10 Saloon and Tilly left a lasting legacy beyond their wartime service. Their rugged reliability and adaptability showcased the importance of versatile transport vehicles in modern warfare. Post-war, many surplus vehicles found new civilian roles, contributing to the reconstruction efforts and securing the foundation for the burgeoning commercial utility vehicle market.

The Military Austin 10 Saloon and the Austin 10 Light Utility Truck are enduring symbols of British automotive innovation and military prowess during the Second World War and beyond. From their origins as civilian passenger cars to their transformation into versatile workhorses close behind the battlefield, these vehicles played a small but vital role in supporting Allied forces in theatres of war across the globe. Through their mobility, reliability, and adaptability, saloon and Tilly Austins contributed immeasurably to the success of military operations and the welfare of front-line troops.

As we reflect on the legacy of the Austin 10 Model 1939, we are reminded of the resilience and resourcefulness of those who designed, built, and operated these remarkable vehicles.

Their story serves as a testament to the enduring spirit of innovation and cooperation that transcends the challenges of war and adversity. Whether on the battlefield or the open road, saloon and Tilly continue to inspire admiration and respect for their contributions to history and humanity.

Successor Vehicles

The use of the appellation 'Tilly' carried on into the late twentieth century in all parts of the UK armed forces, with the Morris Commercial J4 and later the Leyland Sherpa, often in minibus form. The Royal Navy, which had no embedded vehicle assets of its own, unlike its soldiers in the Royal Marines and the other services, was reliant on the civil service Principal Supply and Transport Organisation (Navy) PSTON to provide both the vehicles and drivers.

The Australian Armed Forces similarly carried on this practice but opted to use the appellation UTE taken from the first rather than the latter part of 'Utility'.

Jeep

Tillys were superseded during the war by the American Jeep. The Austin Tilly's off-road capabilities with single rear-wheel drive were so inferior to those of the American Jeep. An interesting detail here is that American Bantam Car Company played a very important role in the development of the Jeep. The first Jeep was a Bantam and the origins of the Bantam Company can be traced back to the British Austin Motor Company. The American Austin Car Company Inc. was an American automobile manufacturing corporation incorporated in the state of Delaware. The company was founded on 23 February 1929, and produced motorcars licensed from the British Austin Motor Company from 1930 to 1934, after it had filed for bankruptcy protection. The company was liquidated in 1935, and the assets were acquired by Evans Operations, Inc. A new company, American Bantam Car Company, was incorporated in June 1936. So, in a strange way the Bantam Jeep has some Austin pedigree. It is therefore amusing that the Austin and other Tillys were superseded by the Jeep.

Austin saloon and Jeep standing beside each other. Both wear markings of the Dutch Princess Irene Brigade. (Author's collection)

Austin Champ

The Austin Champ is, in another way, a successor to the Austin Tilly. The Austin Champ had a Jeep-like appearance but was much more complex. It was produced by the Austin Motor Company in the 1950s. Officially, the army version was 'Truck, ¼ ton CR 4x4, Cargo & FFW Austin Mk.1'. The civilian name 'Champ' was universally applied to the type. The British Army wanted a light truck, specifications for which were issued in the late 1940s, inspired by the Ford and Willys Jeep. It was considered important that a British-made vehicle was produced in order to reduce reliance on American vehicles.

The first three prototypes were designed by the Nuffield Organisation, and these were known as the 'Nuffield Gutty'. Afterwards, thirty prototypes were built by Wolseley Motors Limited under the name 'Wolseley Mudlark' and, after further refinements, the design was formalised as FV1801(a). The Austin Motor Company was awarded the contract to produce 15,000 vehicles. The former aircraft factory at Cofton Hackett, on the edge of Austin's Longbridge plant in Birmingham, was fitted out for the work. The first production vehicle was completed on 1 September 1951. The Champ was produced until May 1956.

A major difference between the two vehicles was the cost involved in production. The Tilly was a cheap, makeshift, early-war solution using an existing chassis and engines already in production and readily available. The Austin Champ was an over-complex and very expensive vehicle. Compared with the Land Rover, a far more successful vehicle, the Champ was essentially an unsuccessful replacement for the Tilly.

Austin A40

After the war, the Austin 10 remained in production until 1947. The Austin Motor Company then switched to the production of the Austin A40. After the war, Ricardo Burzi, the designer of the 1939 model Austin, was responsible for the 'egg-shaped' Austin A30, A40, and A70, as well as the extraordinary A90 Atlantic. More conventional three-box Austin Cambridges and Westminsters followed before Austin was persuaded to turn back to Italy and engage Pininfarina.

Austin Champ. (https://silodrome.com/austin-champ-history/)

Austin A40 Devon from 1951. (Courtesy of kitmasterbloke, Flickr)

Memories and Personal Connections

The Austin, and especially the Tilly, often has a special place in the hearts and memories of different people. Sometimes you are lucky enough as an owner to hear these stories. This is one of the privileges of owning an Austin Tilly. The rich history and impact of this small British Army vehicle goes beyond what many people can imagine.

The Austins are such adorable vehicles, an opinion that everyone generally agrees on. For many Austin owners, this was often the deciding factor in the purchase. But for some people, the bond with the Austin goes deeper. It's personal. This deeper personal connection is often rooted in the past. After the war, an Austin was present in the family and sometimes stayed. Another link is that a father or mother drove an Austin, often a Tilly, during the war.

Wedding Car

After the liberation, many people celebrated with the Allied soldiers. The soldiers sometimes stayed for a few days before moving on and some troops remained even longer after the end of the war. Sometimes love blossomed during that time. These new relationships sometimes led to marriage. On that important day wedding transport was needed. With some white ribbons on the hood handle towards both sides of the window, the Austin Tilly could be transformed into a wedding car.

Impact on Little Boy

That the Austin Tilly can leave an indelible impression became clear during the Operation Market Garden Memorial Tour in 2014. During the tour, my own Tilly was pulled aside. On a long road with many trees lining the roadside, spectators gathered for the procession of

Austin Tilly as a wedding car.
(Tilly Register Archive)

old army vehicles. Suddenly, an old man broke away from the crowd. With slow steps he walked to the middle of the road and held up his hand in a stop gesture. I halted in front of the man, and he made his way over to the driver's side. He stroked the Austin logo on the nose with his hand. Then his hand felt the curve of the fender.

The old man started talking about how happy he was to see this type of vehicle. People usually cannot identify the brand of Austin and sometimes call it Opel or even Citroën. But not this man. He knew exactly what kind of car it was. As a small boy, his father had had one for work just after the war. He and his family rode along occasionally. He would sit in the back on the canvas folding seats, while in the cargo area there were potatoes and other vegetables in gunny bags.

I could clearly see emotion in his eyes. Unfortunately, we had delayed the rest of the vehicles too long and had to move on. While I put the Austin back into gear, the man stepped aside. With a little more gas than necessary, I let the four cylinders hum in neutral for a while. The man clearly enjoyed the sound. He wished us a nice day and, above all, many more miles. The Austin pulled off and in the round mirrors I saw the man slowly return to his place at the roadside. This is one of the privileges of owning an Austin Tilly. The rich history and impact of this small British Army vehicle should not be underestimated.

During Working Life

Ten years later, during the Liberation Task Force event in September 2024, many people came to see the large number of British vehicles that participated. All vehicles received a lot of attention from the public, including the Austin Tilly. At one point I was approached by an elderly lady. Peeking through the open window, she was particularly interested in the dashboard and asked a hundred questions. She came back three more times that afternoon, the last time with her son. From her story it became clear that she used to work at a local garage in the Netherlands where various Austins were maintained. For her work she had regularly walked through the warehouse looking for parts. It was clear that the Austin brought back precious memories for her.

Member of the Family

In the 11 May 2017 episode of National Geographic's *Car SOS*, the team of Tim Shaw and Fuzz Townshend took on a 1941 Austin 10 utility truck. In this case, it was more of a conservation over restoration project. The Austin belonged to a '89 former soldier who had used the Austin on his farm for sixty years. The vehicle had been with the same owner since July 1956.

Preservation and Collectability

Despite the passage of time, the legacy of the Austin 10 Model 1939 GRQ and GYG Tilly endures among automotive enthusiasts and collectors worldwide. Restored examples of these vehicles serve as tangible reminders of a bygone era, evoking memories of sacrifice, resilience, and ingenuity. Through preservation efforts and enthusiast gatherings, the stories of the GRQ and Tilly continue to inspire future generations, ensuring that their contributions to history are never forgotten.

While the Austin Tilly was only produced during the war, the Austin GRQ Saloon was also manufactured after the war. However, to be accurate, this was the later GSI type. As the original GRQs are rare, military collectors and enthusiasts often choose an alternative to the saloon. This could be an older model, such as an Austin saloon from 1938, or a post-war Austin saloon. The latter are then dressed up, inaccurately, in military green and markings. For purists, these are not original military vehicles, but because the supply of original Austins is lagging behind, there are plenty of candidates for these Austins.

Austin Tilly and Austin Military Tourer AP. (Tilly Register Archive)

Being a vehicle with military history, the Austin Tilly has been preserved in small numbers by private individuals. The demand for these small British vehicles has grown since 2000. Thanks to the internet, it has become easier to find parts. Also, the international market has made it possible for military enthusiasts to search for alternative vehicles instead of the more common Jeep, Dodge, and GMC. These vehicles were used in huge quantities by the military in many countries, such as the Netherlands, Norway, and France. When these vehicles became redundant, they found their way into the hands of military enthusiasts. The British Tilly and saloons of all makes are still very popular. Because there were only 29,000 Austin Tillys produced and almost all known surviving Tillys have been registered with The Tilly Register (see below), any vehicles offered for sale sell quickly. Their prices are not the same as for a Jeep, but they continually rise because of their popularity and rarity.

When purchasing an Austin 10, it is important to determine its year of production. This can be done using the chassis number. For Austin Tillys it is possible to even locate the military contract of the vehicle. An additional advantage of knowing the chassis number is that it is possible to pin down the appropriate VRN number (military registration) with a good deal of certainty.

'*The*' Tilly!

For many military and non-military vehicle enthusiasts, the Austin Tilly is '*The*' Tilly. This is due to a number of reasons. There is the greatest chance of seeing a Tilly from the Austin marque as more Austins survive than the other three marques in total. However, the sight of any Tilly in public is fairly rare. The world has become more accessible via the internet where photos and information can be shared on social media. Barriers to purchasing vehicles and parts have reduced thanks to websites like eBay and various specialist military vehicle websites such as Milweb. It has become an international market where free trade is possible.

The reason that Austins are seen more often is quite logical. More Austins were built than the other marques. As mentioned previously, approximately 29,000 were produced. The Hillman was next with 19,500 units, followed by the Standard Tilly at 12,000 (in two different versions), and the Morris at the lowest production of 8,000. In total approximately 68,500 Tillys were built.

To put this into perspective, the American wartime Jeep ran to 500,000 and, after the war, even more were produced under licence by other manufacturers – more than nine times as many. The production of the German Volkswagen Type 82 Kübelwagen ended in 1945 at more than 55,000 units, almost twice the production of the Austin Tilly on its own.

Another reason that relatively many Austins remain stems from the population of Austins on the Maltese islands. In retrospect, these fortunate circumstances were the result of enterprising importers who introduced a large number of Austins in the 1950s and 1960s. Local farmers, gardeners, shopkeepers, and other entrepreneurs bought these Austins for their businesses. The reason why only Austins were imported has never really been explained, other than being the most common Tilly. It is possible that Austins after demobilisation became available in large batches, or parts of the same type were still available. Due to the warm, dry climate and Maltese regulations, Tillys lived on for many

Austin Tilly and Hillman Tilly at Ragley Hall in 2009. (Tilly Register Archive)

years. The Maltese have a reputation for rebuilding/modifying to keep machinery going. Many Tillys were abandoned in the open and became donors for parts. Not much was scrapped until Maltese health and safety stepped in and many of these abandoned vehicles were secreted away in basement garages or yards in the 2010s. There has been a steady trade of exported Austins, in various conditions, to the UK and mainland Europe. This came to an end when the Maltese government adjusted the law and regulations for the export of historic vehicles. The number of surviving Austins is nowhere higher in the world than in Malta. In 2004, in a controversial move, four Austins were exported to the Netherlands, despite the applicable regulations. A loophole found that exporting metal/scrap iron was allowed. The four Austins were far from in running condition, and old engine blocks were delivered separately in an unknown condition. However, in more recent years, a running example has been exported from Malta to the Netherlands. In 2024, a restoration project with extra parts was imported by a Dutch dealer.

The Tilly Register

In 1996, a couple of Tilly owners decided to bring other Tilly owners together into a club. The main goal was to locate surviving examples of Tillys from around the world. Later on, the Austin 8AP Military Tourer was added to the register as the founder member owned all four marques of Tilly, plus a Tourer – the Austin Tilly's smaller cousin. With the quarterly magazine *Tilly Text*, owners and members can learn from each other's experiences, share their knowledge, and even learn some of the vehicle's history. Of course, the magazine includes photos of restorations and rallies. All members can provide newfound photos from the past as sources around the world are still revealing new information and images thanks to the digital era we live in.

The Tilly Register was originally founded by John Simpson and Mike Winter. Both owned all the four marques. Since the beginning in 1996, the register has gained strength with members all over Europe and as far afield as Australia and the United States. When Mike Winter stepped down, his place was filled by Michael Shackleton. He was a regular contributor to *Tilly Text* and a former owner of a Hillman Tilly. Almost thirty years later, the

All four makes beside a VW Kübel and Austin Military Tourer. (John Simpson)

Register has a solid base with the addition of Andy Stroud as treasurer and the author as their webmaster for the website and social media. Many members are involved in sharing photos and information. The magazine has turned from a black and white leaflet in the early years into a full-colour publication, which is also digitally available to members.

The majority of those interested in a Tilly often ask The Tilly Register if any Austin Tillys are available for sale. Plus, of course, the other three marques. The Tilly Register does its utmost, and builds on the success of recent years, resulting in more and more documentation, and the number of 'registered specimens' continues to increase.

It is thanks to The Tilly Register that knowledge about the Austin 10 Light Utility and the other makes of Tillys is secured for the future. Tilly owners can rely on an information network that shares and offers news about all Tillys. Also, it helps new members to reach out to each other. From the 29,000 produced, the register now accounts for 251 examples (though this does include some vehicles that have now been rescued from abandonment in Malta into obscurity – for now). Of course, not all are running, with many in poor condition awaiting the day when their owners have the resources to rebuild them or sell them on to capable owners who enjoy a good restoration project. Most surviving and mobile Austin Tillys can be found in the United Kingdom, Malta, and mainland Europe. This is particularly so in the Netherlands, where the number of Austins grew rapidly from just two in 2002 to fourteen in 2024.

Survivors

Across much of Europe, Austin Tillys have been rescued by military vehicles and are still being restored. In Malta, the majority of survivors are known, with many in running condition. In total, the number of survivors in 2025 was just under 200 Austins. When *Wheels & Tracks* magazine issue 63 was published in 1989, it was thought that only a few dozen survived. At that time, the Tillys were already very collectible.

Austin Tilly survivor, Malta.
(Tilly Register Archive)

Country	1989	2005	2025	Saloons
United Kingdom	30	36	36	4
Netherlands	1	6	14	2
Malta		116	112	
Belgium	1	3	5	
France		1	1	
Sweden		1	1	
Switzerland		1	1	
Kenya	1	1	1	
Sicily		1	1	
Greece		1	1	
Portugal				
Cyprus		1	1	
Czech Republic	1		1	
Germany				

There has never been a count of surviving Austin saloons in the past. During gathering information for this book six GRQs from 1939 were identified. Approximately four saloons could have possibly been wartime saloons, but most surviving saloons are post-war. Most of these vehicles are a standard civilian colour, with black being the most common.

Modellers

For a long time there was no model of any Tilly available. At the beginning of this century, the call for a model of one of the makes of Tilly grew stronger and stronger. Since that time, and with the increasing interest in Tillys in general, several model kits have been introduced. Models are offered in different scales, from 1/72 to 1/48 to 1/35, for a growing public audience to own a miniature Austin Tilly or, indeed, Hillman, Morris, or Standard. Even a 1/16 scale Austin Tilly is rumoured to be in the pipeline.

Restoring the Austin 10

Interest in smaller British Army vehicles has grown since 2000. Jeeps and Dodges are certainly very present in mainland Europe, and the desire for a greater variety of vehicles has increased. This for example, noticeable in the Netherlands. In the period from 2000 to 2020, the Austin Tilly, for example, was imported several times. Some of these vehicles were in running condition but a large number were clearly restoration projects.

So, what attracts MV enthusiasts to a Tilly today? American Jeeps, Dodges, and GMCs are certainly not a rare sight on mainland Europe. An Austin, or other British marque, is still a relatively unusual sight there. Austins in Great Britain have often remained the property of the same family, some handed down from generation to generation, certainly in the case of driving examples. The only way to acquire a Tilly yourself is to find one in need of restoration. This requires more time, knowledge, and often money. Restoring a classic car is rarely intended to make a profit, but is more about owning a dream vehicle. In short, it is real enthusiasts of the Tilly who restore such vehicles back to roadworthiness.

This chapter offers an insight into what to expect when restoring an Austin 10 Saloon or Tilly. Although both vehicles are largely similar, there are some differences for the restorer.

Restoring an Austin 10 from 1939 or 1940 has many similarities, but also a number of important differences. The biggest difference is caused by the history of the vehicle. A saloon is obviously used for passenger transport in daily life. This means that the saloon will have covered many miles, but on paved roads. In addition, the saloon would have been replaced relatively quickly by a successor, possibly the A40. My experience is that surviving Austin 10 Saloons, though used, often remained in their original condition. It goes without saying that certain parts will be worn, but in general the vehicle remains in its original state in terms of the engine, gearbox, and interior. The latter will also show a high degree of wear or, as it is now commonly called, patina.

Austin Utility Truck before restoration. (Tilly Register Archive)

How is restoring an Austin 10 Utility Truck different? This vehicle was already a workhorse during its service in the British Army, and this did not change after the war. It is therefore not surprising that of the 29,000 Austin Tillys produced, only a very small percentage remain. Due to the intensive life of the Tilly both in military service and afterwards in civilian life, the demands that owners placed on these vehicles could be heavy. This was a fairly normal occurrence, especially in Malta. Modernisation of the Tilly required these changes. A worn-out engine, excessive fuel consumption, or the desire for better performance led to engine replacement. This could then be combined with a different gearbox which could involve shortening the driveshaft. For such a new heart of the Austin, the floor and engine compartment may also have to be adjusted. Installation of a new engine and/or gearbox would require a relocation of the engine and gearbox mounts.

After using an Austin Tilly for a long time, the vehicle was often parked on the side out of the way. There it stayed, forgotten, but the owner still cherished precious memories of the vehicle. These memories were probably the reason that the vehicle did not end up in the metal shredder at the local scrapyard.

The Austin slowly but surely would have deteriorated further with the passage of time. Rust would have occurred in several areas and weakened the cabin, fenders, and, finally, the chassis. Fortunately, a dry-stored Austin still shows up regularly. However, these may also have rust and wear in the obvious places where moisture goes to town on the metal, especially the edges of the mudguards where they are mounted to the cabin or body. Wheel arches are a known place for rust to form as well. In addition, water can settle in the punched ribs in the floor, ultimately causing rust damage to the floor.

My experience is that with a saloon, most of the original parts are present, while with a Tilly much has disappeared. That is a disadvantage, but was also an advantage for me at the time. It forced me to search for information about the vehicle. Although manuals and paperwork are generally missing from a purchased vehicle, the manuals still exist. Nowadays many manuals are even available digitally. After finding this information, you will automatically know which parts are missing. The search for those missing parts often

Left: Austin Tilly restoration, floor. (Tilly Register Archive)

Below: Austin Tilly restoration, cabin. (Author's collection)

leads to expanding your personal network. Nowadays, the military vehicle community is no longer limited to your own region or country but extends far beyond national borders. Anyone with a similar vehicle has valuable information. Gathering knowledge about your vehicle is therefore essential for your restoration. Once sufficient information has been found, the restoration can begin. It is not necessary to know everything in advance, because a restoration itself can also provide the necessary information.

In the case of the restoration of my Austin Tilly, I chose to purchase an Austin saloon as a donor. Ultimately, it turned out that the donor was so original that the saloon only supplied a few parts, but mainly served as a reference for the Tilly. Not everyone will have the opportunity to own a reference model. The personal network then comes in handy, because taking photos, taking measurements, and viewing other Tillys or saloons is also invaluable.

Parts of the cars that are often missing include lights. The lamps of the saloon were originally from Lucas, chrome-plated, and quite large. Military lighting was often smaller. During the Second World War, much was standardised, meaning that components such as lighting were used for many vehicles, from motorcycles to heavy trucks. These types of parts have become scarcer since the 2000s. This, of course, unfortunately leads to higher costs.

As the Austin saloon was still being made after the war and parts were therefore still being produced for a longer period, it is fortunately possible to find New Old Stock parts for a restoration. Even when parts are not available, a number of options for parts are possible. It is possible to copy certain parts. Not everyone has the opportunity or knowledge to do this, but fortunately there are talented people and companies that do produce new parts. For example, the original rubber gear cover is now copied from fibreglass. Some parts can be copied by means of brass casting. Another option is to use parts from other brands and sometimes even newer vehicles. For example, the ball joint for the door hinges of a Land Rover is also suitable for the Austin. It is a practical solution to replace parts when the original cannot be found. However, these parts are often also used in other classic cars from well-known brands. Lucas switches, for example, were used on the dashboard and, many years later, were still used on the Austin Healey sports car. The result is that parts for a car from a higher price range also cost more. Therefore, keep as many of the original parts as possible.

Austin Tilly waiting for a restoration in Malta. (Tilly Register Archive)

Points of Attention

The structure of the Austin Tilly comprises a combination of wooden frames, like the A-style, and metal sheeting. In addition to the previously mentioned rust problems, there are other areas that may require attention when restoring the Tilly.

During the restoration process it is important to properly record what comes from where. Every part must be reassembled in the same place during restoration, and dismantling with care is equally as important.

The Floor

The Austin does not have a chassis, so the floor construction must be strong enough. For this purpose, several ribs and metal beams may have been added to the floor in different directions. A floor that lacks strength can deform. Sometimes this is not visible to the naked eye, but after mounting the various body parts it appears that connection points are no longer at the same height. Therefore, make sure that the floor is straight.

Austin Tilly restoration.
A rolling chassis with the cabin, but still without the rear body. (Author's collection)

Austin Tilly restoration.
A rolling chassis with the cabin and the rear body. The engine compartment is still empty. (Tilly Register Archive)

The Load Area

A deformed floor will certainly become visible when installing the loading area. The loading floor and side panels also have their own points to be aware of. There is a convex recess on the inside of the wheel arches. The metal panels are bent around a wooden framework. Originally, the wooden framework was installed first, after which the metal was added. It should also be possible to position the cabin and the wooden cross beams first, and then the sides. Make sure that the comparable points are at the same height.

Chassis Number

It is important to get the Austin registered after restoration, to include the chassis number. In several countries, such as the Netherlands, the chassis number or identification number must be stamped in the chassis. A loose data plate riveted to the chassis does not meet the requirements. Originally, the chassis number is on the bulkhead in front of the cabin. This small data plate does not meet the requirements of the authorities.

Austin Tilly restoration, cargo area. (Tilly Register Archive)

Austin Tilly restoration, cargo area. (Tilly Register Archive)

Above: Austin Tilly restoration. Austin in green paint, ready for further assembly. (Tilly Register Archive)

Left: Austin saloon restoration. During the build the Austin gives a hotrod vibe when the mudguards are not in position. (Author's collection/J. Bonthond)

BODY REMOVAL U/2

Fig. 2.
The Saloon body attachment points are indicated by the arrows

Right: The schematic shows how the body of the Austin saloon is bolted on the chassis. (Author's collection)

Below: Austin saloon restoration. (Author's collection)

Fig. 1.
The actual positioning of all attachment points of Utility is shown in the centre illustration, with close-up detail in each of the associated inset drawings.

Left: Schedule from Austin manual showing the floor construction of the Austin Tilly. (Author's collection)

Below: General arrangement of the Austin 10 Utility Truck. (Author's collection)

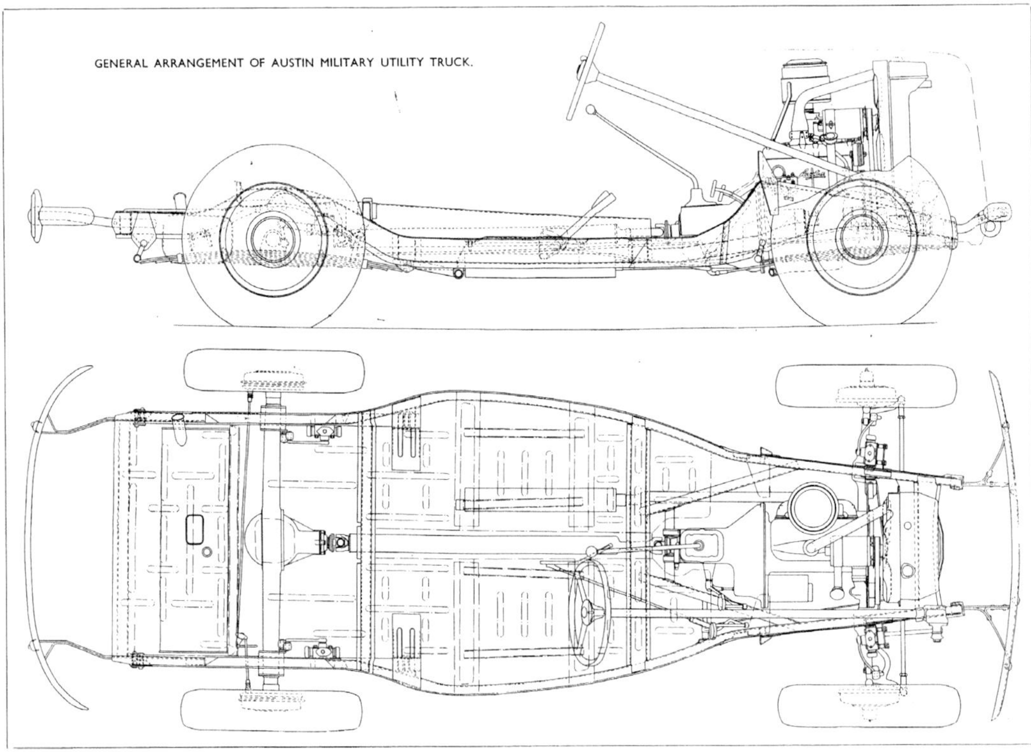

Cost for Restoring

The price of a GRQ Saloon was £185 in 1939. After the war, the Austin Motor Company sold the GSI Saloon for £330 plus £92 purchase tax. After use by the army, the Tillys became available via demob for just £99.

Today, the Austin 10 Saloon and Tilly have a different value. The MV enthusiasts and lovers of civilian classics have created a completely different market. Certainly, for Tilly owners, it is a supplier's market, because the demand for Tillys and saloons is higher than the supply. The supply has decreased, but the interest in these compact and attractive-looking vehicles has increased considerably. Tillys do not come onto the market that often, and those that do are sold quickly due to the high interest.

To purchase an authentic roadworthy Austin Tilly, the price starts at £25,000, depending on condition. Compared with a Jeep, this price is lower, which also makes these vehicles more attractive. For a restored saloon, the price varies between £6,000 and £10,000, although outliers are, of course, always possible. In 2017, a Tilly was offered for 35,000 euros. Ultimately, this Austin Tilly was also sold. It should be noted that this was a full-body-removed restoration, and not an older restoration.

For those who have the opportunity to purchase a restoration project, and can carry it out themselves, the purchase price can be a lot lower. A Tilly in need of total restoration can initially cost between £3,000 and £6,000. Then comes the purchase of materials and missing parts, plus the fabrication of many missing parts. Some parts are also found in more expensive brands, such as Jaguar, which can make them more expensive.

Roughly speaking, a full-body restoration requires hundreds, or even thousands, of man hours. Then there are the spraying costs and, for the saloon, the interior headlining work. Purchasing a restored and running vehicle is the economically sensible choice. Fortunately, there are enough enthusiasts who choose to save and restore a vehicle. They are willing to make the investment this requires. An advantage of restoring an Austin is the knowledge and connection to the vehicle. The vehicle is not an object but feels much more than that. An emotional connection is inevitable – unless the priority is to sell it on for profit.

The increase in interest also has consequences for the value of the Tilly. Nowadays, as soon as a Tilly or saloon is offered for sale, the sale quickly becomes a fact. Of course, an exorbitant asking price is not realistic for any vehicle, but the value is still rising for military vehicles.

Driving a Restored Austin

After restoration of the Austins, both the saloon and the Tilly, these vehicles will hopefully be as near new as possible. However, with the specifications of the 1940s, this means that the car can keep up with everyday traffic within a city or village, but on motorways it is a completely different story.

Both vehicles have good road holding and are certainly easy to handle, despite the lack of any power steering. As mentioned in the brochure, the visibility in the saloon is certainly sufficient. However, visibility is somewhat limited through the two rear windows.

This is different with the Austin Tilly. With a larger door and therefore a larger window, the side view is more than sufficient and with mirrors it is also reasonable along the

The view from the passenger side of an Austin is just lovely. (Corrie Oostdijk)

vehicle. However, with the canvas tilt fitted, visibility is restricted. Driving with an open rear tarpaulin is therefore recommended in order to maintain sufficient visibility using the interior mirror. My own preference is to drive without the tilt if possible.

The slightly higher Tilly can accept different tyres, but this also varies per model. Different brands can be used. As manuals and photos from the Second World War show, it was common to use all-terrain tyres, but also radial tyres on the front. Because the Austins both have rear-wheel drive, this is a logical option. Jeep tyres can also be used on the Austin Tilly. With radial tyres, the saloon has smooth handling and the suspension ensures a comfortable ride. With the lower ground clearance, the saloon is firmly on the road.

The synchronised gearbox generally stands the test of time. The Tilly does have known issues with third gear. When driving with the accelerator pressed, there is no problem with third gear. Only when the throttle is released can the Tilly spontaneously end up in neutral. This makes driving more difficult, especially around corners and roundabouts.

The gearbox generally shifts very smoothly on both Austins. It is synchronised and therefore without double de-clutch. However, of course, the latter is allowed. Shifting from first to second gear is quick and also to third and, finally, fourth gear, is relatively swift. The Austins drive smoothly in fourth gear and the top speed is between 45 and 50 mph. My experience is that the restored Austin Tilly can drive at 50 mph more easily than the saloon. However, long distances at cruise speed are certainly not recommended.

As there are a relatively small number of roadworthy survivors left, both vehicles certainly attract attention from the public and other military vehicle enthusiasts when participating in a rally or static show. The chance of encountering a mobile Austin saloon is even smaller than an Austin Tilly.

The majority of the public will not recognise the make or logo, even though it is on the grille – at least not in mainland Europe. The fact that it takes a while for people to recognise the vehicle is also part of the charm of the Austin. As a result, an Austin is often a conversation starter. Particularly with the Tilly, the combination of the sturdy rear with the canvas tilt and the fine round shapes of the mudguards, nose, and cabin are eye-catchers. There is something sweet and cool about it. This may also be another reason why interest in Tillys in general has increased in recent years.

One of the oldest Austin Tillys at the Wings and Wheels event in Belgium in 2014. Note the BEF markings. (Author's collection)

Austin saloon at a rally in the Netherlands in 2014. (Author's collection)

Above: Austin Tilly at a static show in the United Kingdom. (Tilly Register Archive)

Left: Austin 10 Saloon during Liberation Day, 5 May 2025, in the Netherlands. (Arjan van Prooijen)

Austin saloon at a rally in the United Kingdom. (Kevin Lockyer)

Austin Tilly at a rally in Nijverdal in the Netherlands. (Radek Marcin)

Austin Tilly at Veghel during XXX-corps 2025. Note that the front tyres have a different profile to the rear tyres. (Author's collection)

Austin Tilly with bonnet open. (Tilly Register Archive)

Austin saloon at XXX-corps 2024 at Leopoldsburg, Belgium. (Author's collection)

Two Austin Tillys at XXX-corps 2024 at Leopoldsburg, Belgium. Note the different tyres, tilt, and headlights. (Author's collection)

Restored Austin Tilly in front of Nadur Parish Church, Gozo. (Tilly Register Archive)

Example of a post-war Austin saloon as a military staff car. The latest hubcaps are even pressed with an 'A' for Austin, which earlier hubcaps did not have. (Author's collection)

Austin Tilly at a parade. (Tomas Higgins)

Austin 10 Saloon at a parade. (Tomas Higgins)

Maintenance in Modern Times

These Austins were made in a completely different time, in which regulations and technology were not as advanced as they are today. After eighty years, the technology in a number of parts is so different that something from that time would no longer be allowed. A brake system on all wheels by means of a mechanical rod system is an example of this. However, I can report that this brake system works well, provided it is properly adjusted.

Adjusting the brakes is actually a lot easier than many other vehicles and can be done by the owner. The right tools, a 4/16 spanner and a jack, are all that is needed to complete this job. By lifting one wheel off the ground at a time, the adjustment can begin. With the spanner, turn the adjusting nut on the back of the wheel drum clockwise. A turn of the wheel indicates whether the brake lining is already slightly against the brake drum. In this way, you can adjust all the brakes yourself to ensure that the car brakes evenly.

It is also straightforward under the bonnet, and everything is easily accessible. Maintenance such as replacing the diaphragm in the fuel pump, cleaning the carburettor, or adjusting the brakes can be carried out in half-an-hour to an hour. With the help of one of the manuals, this can actually be carried out by anyone who is not afraid to get his or her hands dirty.

This last aspect is, in addition to driving a classic or old-timer, the charm of this type of vehicle. The care, TLC, and driving is so basic that you can do it yourself. This way you get to know more and more about your vehicle.

Above: Adjusting brakes during an event is easy with just a spanner and a carjack. (Author's collection)

Right: Adjusting brakes according to the driver's handbook. (Author's collection)

C. **INSPECT FOR WEAR AND ADJUST IF NECESSARY, UNDER SUPERVISION WHEN POSSIBLE.**

1. **Brake Adjustment.**

As the brake linings wear, the foot pedal travel will gradually increase. When a point is reached where the pedal travel exceeds about three inches before solid resistance is obtained, the brake shoes must be adjusted.

The Arrow indicates a Front Brake Adjuster.
There is a similar adjuster on each rear brake.

On the opposite side of the drum whence the operating rod protrudes will be seen the square-ended brake shoe adjuster, indicated by the arrow in the illustration. This can be turned a notch at a time, which can be felt and heard and is the engagement of the four flat sides of the cone on the inner end of the adjuster engaging with the plungers which support the shoes. Turn the adjuster in a clockwise direction as far as it will go. The brake shoes are then hard on and the adjuster should be turned back one notch to give the shoes the necessary clearance from the drum.

Each drum should be treated similarly, and it is not necessary to jack up the wheels.

After adjustment is completed, press the brake pedal down as hard as possible once or twice in order to centralise the brake shoes in the drums.

It is important that no attempt should be made to adjust the brakes with the handbrake on.

Use $\frac{3}{16}$in. spanner.

Appendix A

Technical Specifications for the Austin 10

	Saloon	Light Utility Truck
	GRQ or GR/Q	GYG or GY/G
Type	Car, four-seater, 4x2 Saloon	Car, two-seater, 4x2 Light Utility
Engine	Austin G3-222AB	Austin G3-222AB
Bore	2.4995 in	2.62 in
Capacity	1,125 cc	1,237 cc
Power	32 hp at 4,200 rpm	28.7 hp at 3,500 rpm
Torque	66 Nm at 2,250 rpm	66 Nm at 2,250 rpm
Compression	6.52 : 1	6.52 : 1
Gearbox	Four speed	Four speed
Electrical	12 volt	12 volt
Suspension	Leaf-springs	Leaf-springs
Brakes	Mechanical with rods Girling	Drum brakes, mechanical with rods Girling
Wheelbase	7 ft 9.75 in	7 ft 9.75 in
Tyres	16 x 5.00 E.L.P. on 3.00 W.B. rim	16 x 6.00 E.L.P. on 4.00 D. rim
Length	158 in	156 in
Height	64 in	63 in
Width	58.5 in	74.5 in
Weight	2,240 lb	2,212 lb
Ground clearance	6.75 in	8.5 in
Petrol tank capacity	6 gallons	8.5 gallons

Appendix B

List of Contracts

Contract	Type	Date	Numbers	Chassis Numbers	WD Numbers	Notes	Modifications
V2649	GRQ?				M34402	CR16	
V2718	GRQ?		12		M36018-M35029	CR37	
V2809	GRQ?				M353355-353359 M35246-35264		
V2821	GRQ?				M34239		
V2979	GRQ?		6		M36004-36009		
V3087	GRQ?				M37115 till undefined		
V3183	GRQ?		4		M37476-37479		
V3331	GRQ?		4		M3811352-3811355	CR100	
V3349	GRQ?		19		M3811064-3811082	CR97	
V3381	GRQ?				M39936 till undefined		
V3467	GRQ?		11		M3916494-3916504	CR96	

(Continued)

Contract	Type	Date	Numbers	Chassis Numbers	WD Numbers	Notes	Modifications
V3887 or 294/V/ V3887	GYG	18-3-1940	1,757	Typical 190735 (M4163993) 191346 (M4169976)	M4163993-	Serials not allocated in chronical order according to chassis numbers Last two cars diverted Catalogue Reference (CR) 52 without water pumps and CR56	Early features included: Wooden tailgate. Wooden toolbox lids. Tilt with top opening and five windows. Three different hoops plus link struts for front/centre. Hubcaps on wheels. Electric trafficators on both sides. MD143 headlights (large civilian style) on both sides. Exhaust exited on right under driver's door. Rubber gearbox cover. Civilian-style front seats/padded rear foldable seats. From 190497 introduced without water pump on G3-106AB engine. From 191528, G3-123AB engine with water pump and thermostat, revised cylinder head and new front engine support frame. From 192577, Lucas MD140/1 headlamps From 194176, revised spring shackles
V3881	GRQ?				M3812111		

V3928	GYG	3-6-1940	1,691	Typical 193573 (M4322369) 194788 (M4324730)	M4323340-4325030	CR61	From 194808 gearbox improvements (also 194730-194787)
V4014	GYG	17-6-1940	7		M4323380-4325030	Shipped to India. CR68	
V4065	GYG	19-7-1940	2,193	Typical 19561 (M4423356) 196040 (M4423959)	M4423021-4425213	CR64	From 195055, revised body side panels, tilt hoops and brackets, tilt cover, and dividing curtain. Pressed steel tailboard From 195688, LH wheel studs with left-hand thread (instead of earlier right-hand thread). From 195734, single MD140/1 headlight on Left-hand side. From 196087, G3-146AB engine with revised cylinder head (engine 201588) and from engine 207327, new water pump.
V4091	GYG	2-8-1940	750	Typical 197920 (M4439486	M4439009-4339758	CR66	
V4112	GYG	21-8-1940	1,000	197173-199465	M4467067-4468066	For RASC CR70	From 199519, bolted hinge supports on windscreen.

(Continued)

Contract	Type	Date	Numbers	Chassis Numbers	WD Numbers	Notes	Modifications
V4143	GYG	13-9-1940	3,000	Typical 199578 (M4485979) 200761 (M4488897)	M4485898-44688897	CR69	New tail lamps, sidelights and axle convoy light. Stop lamp deleted.
V4181	GYG	2-11-1940	1,500	Typical 199604 (M1135478) 203307 (M1135990)	M1135313-1136812	For RASC	
V4374	GYG	12-12-1940	1,176	Typical 205175 (M1137392) 205337 (M4533861)	M1136813-1137612 M4533513-4533888	For RASC For ROAC CR75	From 204247, G3-161AB engine, new dynamo (e/n 207685 on). Revised instrument panel. Single headlamp with blackout mask (Lucas L-WD-H1) left side only. From 206401, G3-178AB engine (e/n 209501 on) with new air cleaner, dynamo, and voltage control board. Revised instrument panel. Trafficators replaced by single manual arm (LH only). Simplified tilt with no top opening and only single rear window. From 207685, new dynamo. From 207950, water pipes with rubber connections.

							From 207989, revised front axle bumpers. From 208273, revised mudflaps identical on both sides (previously handed). From 208762, canvas instead of rubber gearbox cover and leather cloth gear lever cover.
V4386 *	GYG	1941					
V4809	GYG	17-1-1941	2,437		M113613-1138112 M4672171-4674107	For RASC FOR ROAC CR82	
V4886 *	GYG	1942					
V4891 *	GYG	1942					
V5006 *	GYG	1942					
V5015	GYG	4-2-1942	1,250	209501-210750	M4886340-4887589	Originally for 5,000 vehicles, but balance covered by V1361.	From 209501, front hubs with plugs instead of grease nipples. From 209698, revised front seats with sheet metal backs. From 209889, stretcher rails and tailgate stays. Fitting kits for earlier vehicles. From 210751, G3-210AB engine (e/n 215001 on) with improved crank. From 211217, revised metal tool boxes and lids.

(Continued)

Contract	Type	Date	Numbers	Chassis Numbers	WD Numbers	Notes	Modifications
							From 212675, split-top cab. Revised body sides, header board, rear seats. Interior window and pillar mouldings deleted. From 213058, revised exhaust system and tailpipe exits on the left.
V5170	GYG	3-4-1942	1	2090338	M4575826	Department of Tank Design CR88	
V5193	GYG	20-4-1942	2,000	214901-216900	M5287341-5289340	CR89	
V1361 23/1361	GYG	30-10-1942	3,750	210751-214500	M4887590-4891339	Originally part of V5015. CR113	From 217001, G3-222AB engine (e/n 227012-234633). With revised thermostat and radiator.
V13326	GRQ?		14		M36215-36228		
S1444 or 294/23/ S1444 Or 23/14444	GYG	28-10-1942	5,250	217001-22200 Typical: 218573 (M5396213)	M53394641-5400040	Originally for 6,000 vehicles CR118	Revised distributor from e/n 229592. From 221319, road wheels with flanges. From 221771, revised prop shaft. From 222096, revised rear brake housing.
S1973 *	GYG	1943	2				
S2581 *	GYG	1943	2			CR123	
S2806 *	GYG	1943	1				

S3072 *	GYG	1943	50				
S3630 *	GYG	1943	1				
S4201 *	GYG	1943	2				
S4674 *	GYG	1943	1				
S4177 *	GYG	1944					
S4643 *	GYG	1944	200	223001-223200			
S5469 *	GYG	1944	2				
S6567 * 23/6567	GYG	1944	500				
S6746 *	GYG	1944	2	216962 and 216963			
S6935 *	GYG	1944	1	216964			
S7442	GRQ	1944	1,800	223201-223206 225001-226794	M5880012 - 5881811	CR146	
S8556	GYG	17-1-1945	1,200	228006 onwards. Typical 228069 (M6233819)	M6233756-6234955	Curtailed after 655 vehicles at M6234454 (not all numbers used). CR153	
S8556	GRQ	17-1-1945				Part contract for saloon CR153	
S8767	GRQ	1945	100		M61922862-6192961	CR154	
S1098	GRQ	1945	400		M 6276786 - 6277185	CR168	

Sources

Historic Military Vehicles Directory, B. H. Vanderveen, 1972
Military Transport of World War II, C. Ellis and D. Bishop, 1975
British Military Trucks of World War Two, L. Freathy, 2013
British Army Vehicles, D. E. Jane, 1994
The Observer's Fighting Vehicles Directory WW2, B. H. Vanderveen, 1989
British Cars of the Early Forties, Olyslager Auto Library, 1974
Allocation by Central Census 'B' Vehicle W.D. Numbers door, Rob van Meel
Tilly Colours, Door, M. Shackleton, 2010
The Book of the Austin Ten, Pitman's motorist Library
Army Wheels in Detail, Austin 10HP Light Utility, Petr Brojo, 2010
The Tilly Register
Allied Military Vehicles, Collection No. 1 1941–1946, Brookland Books, 2001
Allied Military Vehicles, Collection No. 2 1942–1944, Brookland Books, 2000
British Car Magazine (Tilly)
British Car Magazine (Saloon), July 2005
Wheels & Tracks, No. 63, Battle of Britain Prints International Ltd, 1998
Military Machines International, December 2009
Tilly Text, Austin Special, January 2005
Historic Military Vehicles Forum
www.austinmemories.com
mafva.co.uk